THE ICE PILOTS

THE

ICE

FLYING WITH THE MAVERICKS

PILOTS

OF THE GREAT WHITE NORTH

MICHAEL VLESSIDES

Douglas & McIntyre

D&M PUBLISHERS INC.

Vancouver/Toronto/Berkeley

12 13 14 15 16   5   4   3   2   1

Douglas & McIntyre
An imprint of D&M Publishers Inc.
2323 Quebec Street, Suite 201
Vancouver BC Canada V5T 4S7
www.douglas-mcintyre.com

Cataloguing data available from Library and Archives Canada

ISBN 978-1-55365-939-6 (trade paperback)
ISBN 978-1-55365-940-2 (ebook)

Editing by Trena White   LBI JAN 2 0 2012
Copy editing by Peter Norman
Cover and interior design by Heather Pringle and Peter Cocking
Cover photography by Ed Araquel, courtesy of Omni Film Productions Limited
Printed and bound in Canada by Friesens
Text printed on acid-free paper
Distributed in the U.S. by Publishers Group West

We gratefully acknowledge the financial support of the Canada Council
for the Arts, the British Columbia Arts Council, the Province of British
Columbia through the Book Publishing Tax Credit, and the Government
of Canada through the Canada Book Fund for our publishing activities.

For those who have ever dreamed,
or dared, to fly…

CONTENTS

INTRODUCTION

At forty degrees below zero, the Fahrenheit and Celsius scales converge. Above and below that point they are strangers, relying upon a complex mathematical formula to bring them into unity with each other. It is only at that single spot that they share the same space, carry the same meaning.

At forty degrees below zero, human flesh that has the acute misfortune of not being covered with protective clothing begins to freeze in mere minutes. The cold air triggers a physiological response focusing on one lofty goal: survival. Capillaries and veins near the skin's surface shrink violently. Blood moves to the body's core in an attempt to protect vital organs.

Yet as valuable as this response may be to keeping us humans alive, it doesn't do much to safeguard some important body parts from the ravages of the extreme cold. Indeed, reduced blood flow to the hands and feet can be dangerous, since blood is the body's primary heating fuel. As blood flow decreases, the chances of frostbite increase.

As the temperature of the skin falls below the freezing point, ice crystals begin to form in its cells, killing them along the way. In its earliest stages, this is called "frostnip," a relatively benign condition that may see a few layers of skin eventually die and slough off, later to regenerate. With continued exposure to the cold, however, the freezing deepens and the damage to fragile flesh increases. True frostbite ensues.

In second-degree frostbite, the skin freezes solid. Blisters may occur a couple of days later, eventually hardening to an unholy blue-purple or black colour. In less severe cases the blisters will eventually peel off (an extraordinarily painful process in its own right), revealing layers of new skin underneath.

Leave the flesh exposed to −40° temperatures for even longer, though, and the freezing becomes more extensive. Deep frostbite occurs as the muscles, tendons, blood vessels, and nerves freeze solid. The skin becomes hard and waxy; the ability to use the area is lost—perhaps forever. Nerve damage is commonplace.

In those severe cases, the only remedy is amputation, as gangrene sets into the now-dead flesh. Entire digits blacken and begin to shrivel, a process sometimes accompanied by a foul-smelling discharge. If the frostbite goes completely untreated, affected body parts may actually fall off.

THAT IS THE CLINICAL view of frozen flesh, one established by scientists working comfortably in their laboratories and offices as they sipped warm mugs of tea or coffee. Yet it is certainly not the only view. Just ask the Ice Pilots.

The Ice Pilots. Since its premiere on November 18, 2009, the television documentary series *Ice Pilots NWT* (commonly shortened to *Ice Pilots* by its fans) has been giving the world an up-close and sometimes painfully personal view of what −40° feels like through the eyes, ears, hands, and feet of the men and women of family-run Buffalo Airways, a throwback airline based in Yellowknife, Northwest Territories, one of the northernmost cities in one of the coldest countries on the planet.

Throwback airline? Indeed. Buffalo Airways operates from a frontier town perched on the edge of a wilderness so vast and remote that only a minute percentage of humankind ever gets to see it, let alone work in it. But what makes Buffalo Airways and *Ice Pilots* the international phenomena they have become are the birds the airline uses to deliver humans and cargo to the far-flung reaches of the North: World War II–era piston-pounding propeller planes that most airlines turned to scrap metal decades ago. These planes—classics like the Douglas DC-3 and DC-4 and the Curtiss-Wright C-46 Commando—once ferried troops and supplies over enemy lines. Now they operate in a different theatre, negotiating the battle lines of blizzards and dwindling fuel supplies in one of the most merciless regions on Earth.

For me, though, Buffalo Airways was a piece of nostalgia, a wisp of memory from a special time earlier in my life. A native New Yorker who came to Canada as an idealistic twenty-five-year-old in the early 1990s, I travelled across this great country to the far reaches of the Arctic, including Yellowknife. And it is impossible to live in the Canadian Arctic without having heard about Buffalo Airways and its crustily iconic leader, "Buffalo" Joe McBryan, who started the airline back in 1970.

Buffalo Joe was a presence in almost every northern community I called home in those years, whether in person or in legend. People said that if something needed to get from Point A to Point B, regardless of the weather or season, Buffalo Joe was the guy to do it. I knew that was true: legends are not

Thanks to Buffalo Joe McBryan, DC-3s such as this one are a common sight across the Canadian North, particularly in Yellowknife, the company's base of operations. With seventy-plus years of history under their wings, the DC-3s are a living testament to Joe's fierce dedication to maintenance and safety.

easily built in a land so rugged it has been known to reduce the toughest of men to babbling fools.

Nevertheless, I'd be lying if I said I didn't entertain the occasional sliver of doubt about the flightworthiness of Joe's fleet of vintage aircraft. Those moments usually occurred in the bay window of my sixth-storey apartment in Yellowknife's Anderson Thomson Tower, which faced the runway of the Yellowknife Airport, a few kilometres away. I would stand there in nervous anticipation, watching a DC-4 attempt to defy gravity and lumber its way over my building, one of the tallest in the Yellowknife "skyline." On more than one occasion I was convinced this was the time the plane definitely, positively would *not* make it over. It always did.

So when presented with an opportunity to dedicate the better part of a year to bringing the inner workings of Buffalo Airways to life in the pages of this book, I leapt. Here was my chance to find out what really makes this quirky-yet-successful airline tick. Here was my chance to explore the rich history of the North and the critical role that aviation has played in weaving its cultural fabric. Here was my chance to get behind the scenes of the show and spend time with Buffalo's characters. And here was my chance to see if I could crack the infamous shell of Buffalo Joe, a man whose temper and stubbornness was the stuff of legend across the North.

1

ARRIVALS

Frostbite wasn't the *only* thing going through my head as I boarded the Bombardier Dash 8 scheduled to take me from the relatively balmy climes of Calgary, Alberta, to Yellowknife, Northwest Territories, one clear mid-January morning. Truth be told, though, it ranked high in the panoply of thoughts swirling through my mind: Will Buffalo Joe like me? Does a wind chill of −42° feel any different to a forty-six-year-old body than it does to a thirty-year-old one? Just how safe is a seventy-year-old plane, anyway?

Those questions, and a hundred others, were bound to be answered during the first of what would prove to be many trips to Yellowknife in the coming months. In the meantime, though, I settled into the modern—if not particularly spacious—comfort of the plane, one of the most popular regional turboprop airplanes in the world.

For good reason. The Dash 8 is a picture of efficiency: depending on the model, the plane will carry anywhere from thirty-seven to eighty passengers at speeds that can eclipse five hundred kilometres (three hundred miles) an hour with relatively little fuel consumption. The interior of the cabin also speaks to modern aviation's obsession with function over comfort. Somehow we managed to park two humans on either side of an aisle large enough to accommodate the flight attendants' snack tray in a fuselage that boasted a diameter of less than three metres (ten feet). In other words, if your seatmate feasted upon a three-bean burrito for breakfast, you'd know about it.

Nevertheless, the seat cushion into which my nether regions nestled was soft and inviting, and the overhead lighting cast a warm glow throughout the aircraft that mimicked the brightening sky to the east. The plane's highly insulated plastic shell deadened the sound of its two turboprop engines. We may have been squeezed in like suitcases on a luggage cart, but we were warm, cozy, and about to cover more than 1,200 kilometres (745 miles) in about two hours.

As the plane lifted off, Calgary's winter landscape began to fall away. The city faded into a prairie patchwork of golden brown and white, dissected into neat squares by the innumerable roads that keep people and commerce flowing along the southern edge of midwestern Canada. Soon we climbed through the ceiling of clouds, and the world below us melted away. All was calm in the upper reaches of the troposphere.

"Ladies and gentlemen, this is your captain speaking. As we begin our final descent into Yellowknife..."

I awoke with a start to the pilot's message; the flight had lulled me into a deep sleep as it hurtled across northern skies. And as my eyes adjusted to the light around me and I gazed through the window, I could tell we weren't in Kansas anymore, Toto.

The checkerboard of the prairie below had been replaced by something more primal. The golden landscape had given way to two colours that wrestled for dominance: charcoal grey and white. The grey occasionally won the battle, as masses of stunted, hardscrabble spruce trees huddled together, forming broad patches of forest in a great, untamed wilderness. It didn't

One of the largest wildernesses on Earth, the Northwest Territories is the raw and often-severe land in which the ice pilots ply their trade. Extreme weather conditions have claimed the lives of many pilots over the years.

take a geographer to recognize that the leaden curves of the forest were mere accents on a backdrop of white.

There was a *lot* of snow down there. This came as no surprise to me, given that I had spent several years of my life criss-crossing the Arctic, from Fort McPherson in the west to Baffin Island in the east. Snow is a part of life in communities that pepper the subarctic and Arctic regions of the world, regardless of the season. What struck me on this flyover, though, was just how much water was sitting underneath all that snow. In every direction, as far as the eye could see, the landscape was peppered with white blots of varying size and shape, gleaming in the cold winter sun, each indicating yet another body of water, from long-forgotten ponds to vast lakes covering thousands of square kilometres.

It occurred to me that, other than the primal landscape of white and grey, there wasn't much else going on down there: no herds of caribou loping gracefully across the frozen land, no eagles soaring over the rocky outcrops in search of prey. Hell, I couldn't even spot a road.

It wasn't until we were descending to within spitting distance of our destination that the trappings of "civilization" began to appear. Snowmobile trails snaked through the forest, bursting onto frozen lakes, where they broadened and braided, only to constrict again on the far side, where they once again plunged into the forest cover. We drew closer, and a road (singular: *one* road) appeared, though from that height it wasn't much more than a grey stripe stretched across the land below.

If anything, the snow served as an acute reminder of my destination. With a population that fluctuates around twenty thousand, Yellowknife is the capital city of the Northwest

Territories (it's also the *only* city in the Northwest Territories), a place where old and new, traditional and cosmopolitan, blue collar and white collar, rough and refined, Native and non-Native, all coexist fairly peacefully.

The city is located some 512 kilometres (318 miles) south of the Arctic Circle, and bears the dubious distinction of being the coldest city in Canada. According to Natural Resources Canada, Yellowknife's average nighttime temperature between December and February is a balmy −29.9°C (−21.8°F). Average. That means that for each day warmer than −29.9°C, there's one colder too. Yellowknife's mean annual temperature is −5.4°C (22.3°F), a figure even more astoundingly cold once you figure that the city also has the sunniest summers in Canada, with June, July, and August racking up a total of 1,037 hours (that's forty-three complete days) of sun each year. It's been estimated that an average Yellowknife winter comprises 191 days, or more than six months.

Yet by the grace of some omnipotent being who realized that my ability to withstand significant stretches of flesh-freezing temperatures had diminished in the years since I left the North, the immediate forecast was on the warmer side of things, relatively speaking. Overnight lows would touch −30°C (−22°F), but daytime highs might actually climb above −10°C (14°F) once or twice. I wasn't breaking out the sunscreen just yet, but I was grateful nonetheless.

If that doesn't seem tropical to you, consider the poor bastards who called Yellowknife home in the winter of 2008. At the end of that January, a cold weather system gripped the North like a vise, making people wonder if this might be the time to consider a move to Vostok, Antarctica, which holds the world record for coldest temperature ever recorded on Earth: –89.2°C (–128.6°F), in 1983. For nine straight days, Yellowknife recorded temperatures below –40°, with wind chills regularly exceeding –50°C (–58°F). The city operated in the hushed haze of a persistent ice fog, a phenomenon that occurs when the water molecules in the air freeze and hang suspended like a ghostly veil.

Entire neighbourhoods were obscured. Mail delivery came to a grinding halt. Schools closed to ensure the safety of students and staff.

IT'S NOT LIKE I haven't seen my share of –40°, though. Like many who call this eclectic place home, I came to the North by a rather unconventional route. Back in the early 1990s, I was happily ensconced in what I then thought was the dream job: working on Park Avenue in New York City, in the Commissioner's Office of Major League Baseball. Several years earlier, armed with a journalism degree from New York University, I had peppered nearly every sports team on the east coast of the United States with letters seeking employment in their public relations departments. Most chose not to reply at all; those that did all said the same thing: thanks but no thanks. All but one, that is.

Major League Baseball informed me that there were currently no jobs available at the office, but I might be interested in applying for their Executive Development Program, started a few years earlier by new commissioner Peter Ueberroth, who wanted to bring young, eager, and talented executives to the industry. One or two recent university graduates were selected every year from a pool of several hundred applicants. Should I be lucky enough to land the position, I would have the rare opportunity to work in almost every department of the

Commissioner's Office, from legal to broadcasting, licensing to player relations, learning everything there is to know about the business side of the game. After about a year, the "executive trainee" would have the opportunity to land a full-time position in the industry, either with a major league club, a minor league club, or one of the various departments in the Commissioner's Office itself. Realizing my chances were exceedingly slim and with nothing to lose, I set to the application form with a vigor I hadn't felt since writing my final term paper for a senior N Y U course called "Human Sexual Love."

I somehow made it through the initial set of interviews, and was shocked to learn I had been selected as one of the finalists. At that point, I realized I was no longer a dark horse in the proceedings and had a legitimate shot at actually getting the job. It was time to break out the big guns. Donning my finest brown wool suit, baby-blue shirt, pink tie, and burgundy wingtips, I headed to the Major League Baseball offices at 350 Park Avenue for my final interview.

The place reeked of tradition, of cool, of a yeah-we-know-we're-badass-but-we-like-to-play-it-casual-nonetheless attitude. I desperately wanted to be a part of it. Black and white photographs of famous players lined the modest walls. I tried to identify each one in turn, just in case the interview included a quiz: *Ty Cobb. Rogers Hornsby. The Christian Gentleman, Christy Mathewson. Babe Ruth.* Yup, I was ready.

As I walked into the conference room—the first one I had ever seen in my life—I likely let out an audible gasp. I was confronted by a cohort of nine Major League Baseball executives sitting around a giant oak table.

Nerves notwithstanding, I must have done something right, because within a week I got the call: I was going to the majors!

With tears of joy running down my face, I called my parents, Traude and Gus, who had immigrated to the United States from Germany and Greece after World War II in search of a better life. I clearly remember telling them that I had just gotten the job that I would have for the rest of my life. "In forty years," I said, "they can give me a gold watch, pat me on the back, and show me the door. I'll be the happiest guy who's ever lived."

How wrong I was.

Only a few years later, seeds of discontent began to sprout somewhere deep inside me. As thrilling as baseball was (how many other people do you know who were *inside* Candlestick Park when the earthquake struck before Game Three of the 1989 World Series?), I started to want something more out of life. The shallowness of my existence was becoming obvious.

I would stand in front of the mirror every morning, wrap my tie into a neat half-Windsor and wonder which client I would have to pretend to like that day. As I began to consider more deeply my place in the universe, I realized I was not cut from the Egyptian broadcloth of Park Avenue. If life held any more great secrets for me, I guessed they would not be found in the hallowed halls of Major League Baseball.

I ended up quitting Major League Baseball and signing on as a volunteer with a small Canadian organization called Frontiers Foundation, which works to this day to provide—among other things—affordable housing in Canada's aboriginal communities. My responsibilities would be simple, yet profound: renovate and/or build houses for some of North America's most disadvantaged people. As altruistic as I felt, I was encouraged by Frontiers' out clause: the minimum commitment was only two months. If I arrived at my posting

Happy moments such as this one became more and more frequent as the months went by, but that didn't mean I was immune to the occasional icy glare from Buffalo Joe.

at some as-yet-unknown hamlet in the middle of Canadian nowhere and realized I had made the biggest mistake of my life, I could always go back to 350 Park Avenue on my hands and knees and beg for my job back.

I didn't need to. For the first time in my life, I was in a completely foreign environment, living with a group of volunteers from around the globe, working outside at a job for which I had no training, no obvious skills. The learning curve—both on the social and professional scales—was high. Not a day went by that I didn't learn something about myself, the world, home construction, or the Native people who called these places home. I loved it.

And so the two-month-minimum commitment window came and went, and I continued doing what felt like the most important work I had ever done. For six months, I bounced around several communities northwest of Sault Ste. Marie, Ontario. If the names Goulais River, Gros-Cap, and Batchawana Bay mean anything to you, you're a better student of geography than I was at the time. And if I thought the challenges of working outside through the Canadian autumn and early winter were tough, I had a lot to learn.

After a brief trip back to New York for Christmas, I was sent out for my second volunteer posting, one that would test my ability to withstand the rigours of weather like I had never before imagined. I was off to Fort McPherson, Northwest Territories, a community of some eight hundred people—primarily aboriginal Canadians, the Tetl'it Gwich'in—that sits about a hundred kilometres (sixty miles) north of the Arctic Circle.

In six months at Fort McPherson I learned more about life and love than I ever had in New York. Here were a people who by most modern-day measures had virtually nothing, but still knew how to appreciate the small treasures of their everyday existence like few people I had met before. If the Northern Lights appeared in the sky, people would stop you on the street to talk about it. When spring came, you would only need to bump into somebody at the grocery store and they would start regaling you with stories of the black ducks they had seen flying over the river earlier that morning. I was pulled into the methodical, comfortable flow of life north of 60, where drinking tea and eating bannock and dried caribou meat were enough to constitute a social event, and a damn good one at that.

Sure, there were problems in Fort McPherson, problems I would soon learn are common throughout aboriginal communities the world over. Alcohol abuse was rampant. There was nothing strange about encountering somebody fall-down drunk on the town's hard-packed dirt roads at any time of the day or night, regardless of the season. Suicide, glue-sniffing, spousal abuse, child abuse, arson, and petty burglary wove a tragic thread through the fabric of life in Fort McPherson. One of my favourite people in town was Robert Zheh (not his real name), who quite literally bore the scars of his discontent as a youth. Half of Robert's face was horribly disfigured, the result of a botched suicide attempt many years earlier. And yet, for all that, I fell in love with the place—and its often brutal weather.

And while the thought of working outside in temperatures that routinely sank below –30°C (–22°F) might have made for many sleepless nights back in my Greenwich Village apartment, I was amazed at how well my body became inured to the arctic environment. Maybe it had to do with the fact that my fellow volunteers and I were all in our early- to mid-twenties, but we threw ourselves into our pro bono work with nary a thought about our well-being. Hammering a nail at –30°C (–22°F) is a painfully drawn-out process (we didn't have the luxury of air nailers), but the mere fact that we were out there, standing on ladders and dangling ourselves off rooftops in cold that most people would otherwise describe as ungodly, was a feat unto itself.

And as the days got longer and the weather began to warm ever so slightly, we appreciated every ray of sunlight that shone on our ghostly white bodies. I distinctly remember working outside in only a shirt and sweatshirt one brilliantly sunny spring afternoon. The temperature was –20°C (–4°F).

AS THE DASH 8 touched down on the tarmac of the Yellowknife Airport, I wondered if my body could handle the rigours of cold the way it once did. It's not like I live in a balmy climate these days; the Rocky Mountain town of Canmore, Alberta, is known for its long, snowy winters. But sitting at a desk in the climate-controlled comfort of my home office is a far cry from pounding nails at thirty below. Frankly, I didn't know how much I could hack it anymore.

The walk from the plane to the terminal building was enough to foment my weather fears into a frenzy. The flight attendant was merciful enough *not* to share the temperature on landing, but it was freakin' cold, and the wind howled across the run-way, whipping the fine layer of snow on the tarmac into fanciful whirligigs. It managed to find its way into every nook and cranny of my clothing, poking intrusively at my flesh with icy fingers. At least, I told myself, the Buffalo Airways hangar will be heated.

A couple of text messages later and I was waiting for none other than Mikey McBryan, general manager and heir apparent to the Buffalo empire, to pick me up. In the interim, I had time to ponder what Mikey might be like in person. Truth be told, I felt like I already knew him, the result of crash-coursing as many episodes of *Ice Pilots NWT* as possible before arriving. From what I could tell, Mikey is an enigma. He is clearly a savvy businessman and the driving force behind Buffalo's emergence onto the world stage as a TV phenomenon. But at the same time, I couldn't help but feel that he's, well, a bit of a frat boy.

And if I expected Mikey to show up at the airport in a late-model sports car befitting his status as a small-time celebrity, I was dead wrong. Instead, a ramshackle white van—resplendently bedecked with the Buffalo Airways logo—rumbled to a stop in front of the terminal. Mikey lumbered out, wearing what I would come to realize may be his only uniform: faded jeans, Buffalo Airways hoodie, and signature ball cap. In fact, in all the time I spent with Mikey in the subsequent months, I don't think I ever saw him without his ball cap. I never worked up the nerve to check the validity of this theory, but I think he may even sleep with the thing plastered to his head.

Round-faced and chubby, Mikey greeted me with a genuine, friendly air that immediately won me over. From what I could tell, this was a man with absolutely no pretense whatsoever, despite his new-found popularity. He does not try to be anything other than exactly what he is: a straight-shooting, endearing, insightful, forward-thinking, dedicated, hardworking guy who loves women almost as much he loves beer. And while Mikey McBryan demands a lot from himself when it comes to work, he does not (unlike his father) project those same demands onto those around him.

It didn't take long before I felt like we were old friends.

Great Slave Lake

GIVEN its English name by the British explorer Samuel Hearne, who first crossed the lake in 1771 and named it for the Slavey people native to the area, Great Slave Lake is the fifth-largest lake in Canada and the ninth-largest in the world (27,200 square kilometres or 16,901 square miles). The lake is 615 metres (2,000 feet) deep in some places, making it the deepest in North America. It's icy cold and frozen for eight months of the year.

There are seven communities peppered around the lake: Yellowknife, Fort Resolution, Hay River, Behchoko (formerly Rae-Edzo), Lutselk'e (formerly Snowdrift), Dettah and N'Dilo (both located just outside Yellowknife).

"Hey, Mike," he said as he walked into the terminal, greeting me like we had done this a thousand times before.

"Mikey!" I cried, perhaps a little too eagerly, considering that this was, after all, our first time meeting face to face.

"Let's go to the hangar," he said, shouldering my heavy, green duffel bag, jam-packed with as much arctic survival gear as I could resurrect from long-ignored boxes in a corner of my basement. The hangar, I soon realized, *is* Mikey's home away from home. Actually, scratch that. If the number of hours spent in a place—including sleeping hours—count for anything, then the hangar *is* Mikey's home, period. His house, perched on the shore of Great Slave Lake's Back Bay, is his home away from home.

ON THE SHORT DRIVE from the airport to the Buffalo hangar, Mikey gave me the lay of the land, Buffalo style. Buffalo Airways started operations back in May 1970, when his father, Buffalo Joe McBryan, bought the operating licence from a man named Bob Gauchie. Since those humble beginnings with only two planes—a Noorduyn Norseman and a Cessna 185—Buffalo Joe and his family have built a unique empire of more than fifty planes, most of which flew during World War II. Instead of buying the latest and greatest aircraft money can buy, Joe McBryan is one hundred percent retro.

As Mikey has been known to say: "Forty years ago, Joe was one of hundreds of people flying these airplanes. Then he woke up one day to find out he was one of the last ones doing it."

It's easy to ask why Joe insists on using seventy-year-old planes, and I believe the answer is twofold. First of all, Joe is a collector of old things. "*Vintage* things," Mikey corrected me. Right—vintage things. The guy loves vintage cars, old signs, retro hairstyles, and vintage planes. Reason number two: it makes financial sense. Old planes—though increasingly difficult to find and maintain due to a dwindling supply of parts and experienced mechanics—are cheap. Buffalo can pay off a DC-3 in a couple months of hard work, something few airlines can boast when they lay out tens of millions of dollars for a new jet.

Yet for all of our talk about Buffalo the company, most of our conversation centred on Buffalo Joe, captain and president of the airline. As we talked, I got a sneaking suspicion that Mikey was trying to prepare me for something, something unspoken that lay between us on the floor of the rattling van, like a polar bear waiting to pounce on a seal. I ignored it and tried to focus on what Mikey was saying so I could be as prepared as possible to meet Joe in a few minutes' time.

"He's always a stress case, always running around and micromanaging one aspect of the business or another," Mikey said of his father, a man whose legend in the Canadian North has grown to untold proportions thanks to the success of *Ice Pilots NWT*.

"He thrives on stress, eats it for breakfast, lunch, dinner. And anything going on right now—from a garbage can overflowing in the hangar to whether or not the lights in the bathroom should be left on—he's worried about it. And he picks it; he picks whatever he wants to stress out about that day."

"Doesn't seem like a particularly healthy lifestyle," I threw in.

"Yeah, but it keeps him going," he said. "Look at the guy. He's thin and healthy, but he survives on junk food and adrenaline. He lives like a sixteen-year-old would live, and he hasn't grown out of it."

If anything, Mikey said, my biggest challenge would be to slow his father down long enough to get him to talk to me. "That's why there's hardly anything written about him; he's as elusive as Bigfoot," Mikey said. "How many videos of Bigfoot are there?"

The key is to get to Joe on the weekends, which he spends in Yellowknife with Mikey, instead of at the Monday–Friday home he shares in Hay River with his wife, Sharon. On those days, when the whirl of business has slowed to a manageable level, Joe is at his most relaxed, and therefore, most talkative.

Still, if the stories I'd heard about Joe are true—not to mention the way he'd been portrayed on *Ice Pilots*—he wouldn't be inviting me to dinner anytime soon. Even when I lived in remote Arctic communities thousands of kilometres from Yellowknife, people talked about Buffalo Airways and its nefarious founder. Joe was the kind of guy you wanted on your side if you needed a job done—and done *now*. Hang out socially with the guy? Maybe not. There are stories of new recruits arriving at the hangar on a Friday and leaving for home Sunday morning. Either the TV show has managed to capture every one of Joe's temperamental outbursts, or they happen with alarming regularity.

Still, I was cautiously confident as we pulled up to the Buffalo hangar. I'd met—and cracked—many tough nuts in my day, so Joe McBryan should be no problem at all. I'd regale him with a few stories about my days in the Arctic to win him over, throw in a bit of the ol' Vlessides charm, and soon we'd be shooting the shit like we'd been friends forever. He was already on board with the idea of the book, so it was just a matter of getting him to like me. Piece of cake!

As if on cue, I literally bumped into Joe as we walked through the inconspicuous green metal door that opens into

Purchased from legendary aviator Max Ward, the Buffalo Airways hangar boasts a concrete floor six feet thick, perfect for withstanding the weight of the aircraft and Yellowknife's mercurial weather. The hangar houses several aircraft at one time.

the inner sanctum of the Buffalo Airways hangar. I had no trouble recognizing him. His brown hair was slicked back into a neo-pompadour and showed nary a sign of grey despite the fact that he was approaching seventy. His face was not as wrinkled as I thought it would be, his teeth surprisingly white. His clothes were unassuming and spoke to the casual places he's called home his entire life: dark jeans and a flannel shirt, a red plaid flannel lumberjack jacket on top. He wore his watch backwards on his right wrist.

As Mikey introduced us, I sensed trepidation in my guide's voice. "Dad, this is Mike. He's the guy writing the book."

"Book…" Joe growled, eyeing me suspiciously. "What book?"

Uh-oh.

Mikey's phone rang and he turned away, now deep in conversation with pilot Devan Brooks.

Joe's suspicious look bore holes into my skull, out the other side, and through the fuselage of the DC-3 lurking behind me. "I never agreed to no fuckin' book."

Oh boy.

I was drowning, my hands stretched helplessly toward the disappearing surface above. The light was fading, my watery grave becoming darker.

Joe broke the silence as I tried to mumble something intelligible.

"Do you have an aviation background?" he asked.

"Well, not really. But I have flown a bunch of times, if that counts for anyth—"

"Then it's gonna be tough writing that book," he cut me off. "I'd strongly reconsider it if I were you. I don't have time to educate people, especially non-aviation people."

"Actually, this book is not really going to be a technical manual, but more of a story about—"

"You go in that office of mine, and every book on the shelf is an aviation book," he continued over me. "I read a lot of books to see how accurate they are and how they spread the credit and the blame around. And every one of them is a piece of shit. I buy the books only for time, places, and data."

Mikey must have seen the beads of sweating forming on my brow, because he finally ended his phone conversation and turned back to throw me a life preserver. Joe took no notice.

"I'm very busy right now," he continued, "and there aren't a lot of people helping me. They're finding me a lot of problems to solve because they can't handle them themselves. So I'm not really in the best mood to be writing a book."

Mikey joined me in mumbling and fumbling, trying to explain things to Joe. "It's really about timing," Mikey said. Joe had turned on his heels and was heading for the far side of the hangar. Clearly, he'd had enough of our conversation. "Just think about it!" Mikey called after him.

An uneasy silence hung between us as we watched Joe march away. "That went well," Mikey said. "Better than I thought, actually."

2

THE INNER SANCTUM

Having temporarily removed Joe from my list of potential interview candidates, I was faced with more free time than I had originally bargained for, but at least it gave me an opportunity to explore the inner sanctum of Buffalo Airways.

I'd never been inside an airplane hangar before, and the sheer volume of the place bordered on overwhelming. The hangar itself stretches 45 metres by 45 metres (150 feet by 150 feet), enough to house half a football field. The roof soars more than fifteen metres (fifty feet) overhead, curving slightly higher from its east and west walls to the highest point directly in the middle. On either end of the hangar are adjoining buildings that house Buffalo's offices, various parts and storage rooms, the passenger waiting room, and the small but wildly successful shop that sells Buffalo merchandise.

Huge though the place may be, one thing becomes immediately apparent: Joe McBryan runs a tight ship. The hangar is the picture of efficiency, a testimony to a near-obsession for Buffalo Joe: safety. An assortment of racks and stands peppers the hangar, each neatly festooned with a variety of airplane parts. Everywhere I looked, men were perched on rolling stands, elbows deep into the guts of an airplane. The walls were dripping with racks of belts, parts, and papers, all organized into tidy little rows for easy identification.

Two enormous steel doors, each twenty-one metres (seventy feet) wide and fifteen metres (fifty feet) high, guard the entrance to the hangar. A series of windows near the top of each door flooded the room with natural sunlight. The place was abuzz with activity: bright, lively, and full of purposeful energy. Everybody, it seemed, had a job to do, knew what it was, and got to it without hesitation or question.

As if trying to absorb the variety of strange and wonderful sights bombarding my eyes was not enough, I couldn't help but notice that my olfactory system was also doing jumping jacks. The smell is not *bad* by any stretch of the imagination. But it is distinctive. It's a smell of oil and rubber, of sweat and grease, and of hard-working men in coveralls manipulating pieces of metal to do what they were designed to do: to fly.

TO FLY. HUMANKIND has long dreamed of defying gravity and taking to the skies. The Chinese are said to have discovered that kites could fly, as early as 400 bc, a discovery that jump-started humans into thinking that we could fly too. Around that same time, a Greek philosopher, scientist, and states-man named Archytas is said to have created what is widely

The Buffalo Airways Fleet

BUFFALO AIRWAYS is the proud owner of fifty-two aircraft, forty-nine of which are registered to the airline and three to the Buffalo School of Aviation, which hasn't run courses in several years.

1 Aeronca Champion: C-FNPJ

2 Beechcraft Baron: C-FULX, C-GBAU

3 Beechcraft King Air: C-FCGE, C-FCGH, C-FCGI

3 Beechcraft Travel Air: C-GIWJ, C-GWCB, C-GYFM

7 Canadair CL-215: C-FAYN, C-GBPD, C-GBYU, C-GCSX,
   C-GDHN, C-GDKW, C-GNCS

1 Cessna 185: C-FUPT

2 Consolidated Vultee (Canso): C-FNJE, C-FPQM

1 Consolidated Vultee (Convair): C-GTFC

3 Curtiss-Wright C-46 Commando: C-FAVO, C-GTPO, C-GTXW

1 Douglas C-47 Skytrain (a military variant of the DC-3): C-FCUE

13 Douglas C-54 Skymaster (a variant of the DC-4): C-FBAA,
   C-FBAJ, C-FBAK, C-FBAM, C-FBAP, C-FIQM, C-GBAJ, C-GBNV,
   C-GBSK, C-GCTF, C-GPSH, C-GQIC, C-GXKN

9 Douglas DC-3: C-FDTB, C-FDTH, C-FFAY, C-FFTR, C-FLFR,
   C-GJKM, C-GPNR, C-GWIR, C-GWZS

1 Fleet Canuck: C-FDQJ

3 Lockheed L-188 Electra: C-FIJX, C-GLBA, C-FIJV

1 Noorduyn Norseman: C-FSAN

1 Robinson R22 helicopter: C-FNEO

credited with being the first self-powered flying machine: his bird-shaped, steam-powered model, the Pigeon, reputedly flew over 200 metres (650 feet). In 559 ad, Yuan Huangtou, the son of Chinese Emperor Yuan Lang, became the first person to fly on a large kite when he was forced to jump from the Tower of Ye by Gao Yang, who had usurped power from Yuan Lang. He survived the flight, but was later executed. Europeans began building and flying their own gliders around the ninth century AD.

Most of the work done on human flight in the hundreds of years between the Renaissance and the explosion of aviation research in the eighteenth century took place on paper, with great minds like Leonardo da Vinci dedicating their efforts to a variety of designs. Da Vinci made the first real studies of flight, with more than a hundred drawings illustrating his theories. Da Vinci's best-known aviation-related sketch—the ornithopter flying machine—was never actually built but is the basis for the modern-day helicopter.

The modern era of aviation began in earnest in the late 1700s, as a series of French scientists brought ballooning to the forefront of the public's consciousness. In late November 1783, brothers Joseph-Michel and Jacques-Étienne Montgolfier launched the first hot air balloon with human passengers. King Louis XVI had originally decreed that the flight would be manned by condemned criminals, but a couple of men successfully petitioned for the honour. Jean-François Pilâtre de Rozier and the marquis François d'Arlandes drifted gently in the wood fire-powered craft before coming to a landing in a field some eight kilometres (five miles) away.

With the successful flight of hot-air balloons, work on a steerable "airship" continued throughout the 1800s. These airships were extremely fragile and their existences short-lived, so focus again turned to defying gravity with a craft that was heavier than air, particularly in Europe, where innumerable prototypical airplanes were tested, re-tested, and re-tested yet again.

British aristocrat George Cayley was the first scientist to identify the four aerodynamic forces of flight—weight, lift, drag, and thrust—and their relationship to one another. In 1853, Cayley built a three-winged glider that carried his coachman 275 metres (900 feet) across Brompton Dale in northern England before crashing. It was the first recorded aircraft flight by an adult (Cayley reported having a ten-year-old boy fly one of his planes several years earlier). Frenchman Félix du Temple's *Monoplane* is credited with lifting off of a ski jump run under its own power in 1874, after which it glided for a short time before returning to the ground.

The breakthrough moment our species had been waiting for took place on December 17, 1903. On a humble airstrip near Kitty Hawk, North Carolina, Orville Wright flew the *Wright Flyer*—which was powered by an internal combustion engine—for twelve seconds over a span of 37 metres (120 feet). Various museums and aeronautical associations around the world consider it the first heavier-than-air machine to achieve controlled and sustained flight with a pilot aboard. Later that day, Orville's brother, Wilbur, flew the *Wright Flyer* 260 metres (850 feet) in fifty-nine seconds.

Yet the Wright brothers didn't happen upon their discovery serendipitously. These were dedicated, methodical scientists who took their responsibilities seriously, having designed, built, and tested a series of kite and glider designs earlier in the century before turning their attentions to powered aircraft. They even built a wind tunnel to test their various designs, a step that advanced the science of aeronautical engineering tremendously.

Yet not everyone accepts that the Wrights were the pioneers of modern aviation. On September 13, 1906, in Paris, France, a Brazilian inventor named Alberto Santos-Dumont made a public flight in an airplane he called the 14-bis. Though few people question that the Wrights were first in the air, debate continues about which craft—the *Wright Flyer* or the 14-bis— had the more practical design, and therefore the first "true" airplane. More recently, evidence has been uncovered that suggests an American named A.M. Herring may have made

On December 17, 1903, Orville Wright laid at the controls of the first powered, sustained flight while his brother Wilbur ran alongside him to balance the machine.

the first powered flight, in Michigan in 1898 or 1899. Dozens of other inventors also claimed to have taken short flights between 1900 and 1910.

Regardless of who actually made the first documented flight, the aviation world changed forever after the turn of the twentieth century. Planes were almost immediately incorporated into military service. Italy sent planes on bombing missions during the Italian-Turkish war in 1911–12. Bulgaria followed, using its planes to attack Ottoman positions during the First Balkan War (1912–13). World War I saw both sides of the conflict use planes extensively, both for bombing and reconnaissance.

With the end of World War I, the planet was poised for another step in the evolutionary chain of manned flight. Enter the Golden Age of aviation, a twenty-year period between 1918 and 1939 that saw a host of rapid advancements in aircraft technology. Gone were underpowered biplanes made of wood and fabric, replaced by high-powered, single-wing aircraft made primarily of aluminum.

War has a way of spurring technological advances, and the aircraft industry was no different. World War II caused a huge surge in the development and production of airplanes, with virtually every country involved in the conflict dedicating a significant portion of its resources to developing and building flight-based weapon-delivery systems. The first functional jet plane was flown in World War II (the Heinkel He 178), followed shortly by the world's first fighter jet (the Messerschmitt Me 262), and the world's first jet-powered bomber (the Arado Ar 234). Yet if there's one plane that made its presence felt in the second great conflict, it was a twin-engine piston-pounder

Built in 1942, C-GWZS is one of the Douglas DC-3s that Buffalo Airways uses to fly the scheduled passenger service between Hay River and Yellowknife, Northwest Territories. The plane was the 12,327th DC-3 off the assembly line in California.

whose speed and range changed the airline industry forever. And it was looming right in front of me: the Douglas DC-3.

NOBODY IN THE Buffalo Airways hangar seemed bothered by my presence, so I took the opportunity to wander over to the great metallic beast. Like most modern-day travellers, I have fairly extensive experience with aircraft, but exclusively from an end-user's standpoint. Usher me down the Jetway and I'm quite comfortable finding my seat inside the plastic-and-metal tube that will hurtle me to my destination at a cruising altitude of thirty-five thousand feet. I know how to fold my jacket neatly and stow it in the overhead baggage compartment and can even eat an inflight meal (should I be lucky enough to be *served* an inflight meal) without dribbling half of it on my jeans. And if push came to shove, I could probably even place an oxygen mask on my face without accidentally hanging myself on the rubber tube. But this was different.

Seeing a plane, especially a craft as legendary as the one before me, from this vantage point is a unique experience. Up close and personal, the Douglas DC-3 may well be the most beautiful and enigmatic piece of machinery I've ever seen. Its gleaming aluminum alloy fuselage stretched gracefully toward the front of the hangar, curving gently outward to its widest point, after which it gradually narrowed again as it neared the cockpit. The horizontal stabilizers jutted out abruptly from the back of the craft, filling the foreground. I could make out the dramatic sweep of the main wings off in the distance, the hint of a propeller peeking over the top of each one on this twin-engine beauty.

Yet the plane was not about to reveal all her secrets to me from a distance. I got closer, walking her length and running my hands along her smooth yet dimpled surface, 500,000 rivets bouncing under my fingertips. This plane—like each plane in the Buffalo fleet—is no museum piece, no matter how old it may be. No, this is a working plane, a hardscrabble, down and dirty, bare-bones machine that is the backbone of Buffalo's business.

The "3," as she is affectionately known, shared the same smell that permeated the hangar, though the primary bouquet was that of grease and oil. As I walked toward the front, the plane began to rise overhead and I could actually fit my six-foot-four frame under the fuselage. No museum piece, indeed! A fine layer of shiny black oil coated the underbelly of the craft. Sheet-metal patches large and small interrupted the otherwise predictable pattern of her frame. Each is a testimony to the rich history of this venerable old bird, whether it be hiding a bullethole from World War II or a dent caused by an impromptu meeting with a spruce tree limb on some long-forgotten northern airstrip.

THE DOUGLAS DC-3 is credited with revolutionizing the world of air transportation in the 1930s and 1940s and to this day is considered one of the most significant transport aircraft ever made. The plane was born of a rivalry between two of the most powerful airlines on earth in the 1930s: United Airlines and TWA.

As the Great Depression was tightening its grip on the American economy, both United and TWA were looking to beef up their fleets with Boeing's new flagship 247 aircraft. United managed to lock down an order of five dozen 247s, leaving TWA high and dry until the entire order had been filled, a process that could take years. Not willing to give in quite so easily, TWA turned to pioneering aircraft designer Donald Douglas, founder of the Douglas Aircraft Company, to design and build a plane that would compete with the 247. Douglas's resulting design was 1933's twelve-passenger DC-1, of which only one prototype was built.

TWA asked for a few modifications to the DC-1 (primarily increasing its seating capacity and adding more powerful engines), which led to 1934's more robust DC-2, a fourteen-seat, twin-engine airliner; TWA ordered twenty of the new planes. The DC-2 was so popular that a host of European airlines placed orders as well. They all wanted a piece of the plane that proved modern passenger air travel could be safe, comfortable, and reliable. And while the DC-2 was a fine machine, it still had room to improve. Enter American Airlines CEO Cyrus Smith.

Smith was looking for a "sleeper" plane—one in which passengers could stretch out and sleep on long-distance journeys—to replace American's aging fleet of Curtiss Condor II biplanes, so he convinced Douglas to modify the DC-2, using a pre-order of twenty planes as bait. The new plane was engineered over the next two years, and on December 17, 1935— the thirty-second anniversary of the Wright brothers' first flight at Kitty Hawk—the prototype fourteen-berth DST (Douglas Sleeper Transport) took to the air, followed soon after by its sister dayship, the twenty-one-seat DC-3. American Airlines introduced DC-3 passenger service on June 26, 1936.

With the advent of the DC-3, air travel changed forever. The plane needed to refuel only three times during transcontinental trips, meaning people could fly from one side of North America to the other in as little as fifteen hours. The plane boasted amenities previously unheard of in air travel; passengers enjoyed such luxuries as on-board bathrooms and hot meals. For the first time, passengers could stand up and walk around the plane while airborne.

Thanks to a comfort and convenience previously unknown in passenger air travel, more people took to the skies than ever, and rail travel faced serious competition for the first time. Some airlines realized they could make more money from passenger travel than from shipping mail and other cargo, so it didn't take long before American Airlines' competitors jumped on the bandwagon: over four hundred DC-3 orders were placed almost immediately.

War changed the landscape once again, and the DC-3 was the world's plane of choice to move troops and cargo. During World War II, some ten thousand U.S. military versions of the DC-3 were built, though under different names: the C-47 Skytrain, the c-53 Skytrooper, the r4d Skytrain, and the Dakota. These planes boasted reinforced metal floors, larger access doors, and a towing cleat for pulling gliders. The plane could carry twenty-eight fully equipped paratroopers or as much as six thousand pounds of cargo, which might include a jeep and trailer, or even an anti-tank gun. Yet the Americans were not alone in their love of the dc-3. The armed forces of many countries involved in the war also used the dc-3 to move troops and cargo.

In one famous incident in China, a dc-3 earned the nickname "Whistling Willie, the Flying Sieve" after it was riddled with bullets from Japanese machine-gun strafers. After Chinese labourers patched more than a thousand holes with pieces of canvas, the "3" was deemed airworthy enough to carry sixty-one refugees—far more than its intended payload—to India. The plane encountered a tropical storm en route, ripping the canvas patches to shreds. With nothing to cover its myriad holes, the plane whistled through the air like a screaming banshee for two hours through hostile skies. When it finally landed, an Army major approached the weary pilot and growled: "Why did you bother to radio ahead? We could hear you fifty miles away!"

Production of the dc-3 came to a halt in 1942, but that didn't prevent commercial airlines from adding the planes to their fleets in the years to come. When the war ended in 1945, militaries around the world—particularly the U.S. military—found themselves sitting on more dc-3s than they could ever hope to use. The solution was to convert them back for civilian use and sell them to commercial airlines. This almost unending supply of cheap and easily maintained airplanes helped usher in the postwar air transport industry. In total, 16,079 dc-3s had been built, the majority in California.

Douglas DC-3 Facts & Figures

- CAPACITY: 2 flight crew and 21–32 passengers, depending on seat configuration
- PRODUCTION: 16,079; 10,655 in the United States
- LENGTH: 19.7 metres (64 feet, 5 inches)
- WINGSPAN: 29 metres (95 feet)
- HEIGHT: 5.2 metres (16 feet, 11 inches)
- MAXIMUM SPEED: 346 km/h (215 MPH)
- CRUISE SPEED: 240 km/h (150 MPH)
- RANGE: 1,650 kilometres (1,025 miles)
- EMPTY WEIGHT: 8,300 kilograms (18,300 pounds)
- MAXIMUM TAKEOFF WEIGHT: 12,700 kilograms (28,000 pounds)

OF THE THOUSANDS of DC-3s built more than seventy years ago, approximately four hundred are believed to be still flying, primarily as cargo aircraft, though they are also used in aerial spraying, military transport, sightseeing and skydiving, and as passenger airlines. The fact that it is still in daily use makes the "3" unique among prewar aircraft. Perhaps even more telling is the fact that the plane is used in some of the harshest working conditions on the planet. It has an uncanny ability to land on improvised runways of grass, dirt, and ice (its landing gear can be outfitted with skis), making it popular in remote locations and developing countries, where runways are not always paved. From deserts to jungles to the High Arctic, the DC-3 has been there—and is still there.

Buffalo Joe is among those who stand on the front lines of DC-3 dedication, never wavering from his firm belief that when it comes to reliability and efficiency, little else compares to this aging warbird. The company currently owns thirteen of the aircraft—six of which it keeps running at any one time—spread among its various hangars in Yellowknife, Hay River, and Penhold (Red Deer), Alberta. The DC-3 comprises the largest percentage (27 percent) of Buffalo's current fleet.

Joe will tell you it's one of the most reliable and trouble-free airplanes ever built. That's no surprise, really. One of the most important features of the "3"—a design specification ordered by none other than pioneering aviator Charles Lindbergh, who was a TWA director at the time—is that the plane should always be able to fly on one engine.

Perhaps that's why pilots and mechanics alike are so dedicated to this creaky old bird, a pilot's aircraft if ever there was one. There's a common saying among those who know the plane best: "The only replacement for a DC-3 is another DC-3." Buffalo Joe sees it much the same way, though he adds his unique flair when describing the merits of the plane: "If you really want to experience flight in this life, you have to strap a DC-3 to your ass," he says.

He's right. Though I'll likely never know what it feels like to fly a DC-3, in the months to come I would have ample opportunity to sit in the cockpit of that great groaning beast as she made her way across northern skies. And like Joe says, there is nothing—*nothing*—that compares to soaring above the world's last great wilderness in a plane that once flew clandestine missions during World War II.

Having a DC-3 strapped to his ass is where Joe is in his element. The metamorphosis that occurs in his personality at every Sunday–Friday afternoon is remarkable. Here is a man who carries the weight of running an airline on his shoulders for most of his waking hours. He worries about the safety of his aircraft and the people he calls upon to fly them. He worries about the employees who depend upon Buffalo Airways to pay their mortgages and put food on their tables. He worries about remote northern communities that would be stuck without essential food, products, and services if his planes missed their deliveries. But at his core, Joe McBryan is a pilot, and he is never more comfortable than when he sits down early every morning and late every afternoon (except Saturday) in the cockpit of C-GPNR, C-GWIR, or C-GWZS, the three DC-3s that ply the skies between Yellowknife on the north-central coast of Great Slave Lake and Hay River on its southwestern shore. "It's like night and day," Mikey says, "a complete change of personality. He'll yell and scream all day, and once he gets that over with and gets on that plane, he's happy."

It doesn't take long for even the newest arrival to the Buffalo family to see it. By day, Joe is a hardened businessman, one with exceptionally high demands for the people around him, no matter what position they hold in the business's hierarchy. He rarely cracks a smile, and he prowls around the hangar and adjoining offices like a lion on the hunt. If there's something going on in the business, Joe knows about it, is likely worried about it, and will probably find something about it that needs to be improved. Walk across the tarmac of the Yellowknife or Hay River airports to the stairs of the DC-3, however, and there's a different person waiting for you. Sure, he *looks* like the Joe McBryan you've been scared to bump into in the hangar, but *this* Joe McBryan is busy greeting passengers as they board the plane. He chats with old friends, welcomes them aboard, laughs and smiles as they offer their stories of the day. He is, in a word, *charming*.

And the more I came to know this man, the more I realized that he *needs* to do this. He needs to fly, needs to be behind the controls of the aging World War II beauties to which his name is so closely linked. But he also needs this kind of relaxed, gentle human interaction that he seems to find so difficult at other times during the day. Because while he is loath to show it to the outside world, Joe McBryan is really an ol' softie at heart.

You certainly couldn't tell by his work ethic, though. Buffalo has been offering its scheduled Yellowknife–Hay River service continuously since 1982. Joe flies each one-hour (200-kilometre) leg across the belly of the great lake, leaving Hay River at 7:30 every morning and returning home at 5:00 every evening. That's twelve flights each week, or 624 flights a year. So between 1982 and 2010—give or take the odd missed flight for weather—Buffalo Airways' daily DC-3 airline passenger service flew 17,472 times. Joe McBryan was at the helm for almost all of them.

It makes me wonder if he ever looks forward to a day off or (God forbid!) a vacation. "Why would I go on holiday?" he snapped at me when I asked him when he'd last taken a break for a little R & R. "So I could sit on my ass?"

3

THE KNIFE

aking Joe's words to heart, I made it a point not to sit on my ass, particularly when I was in his presence. Even when I was on my own, I relished the opportunity to explore Yellowknife.

Set on the northern shore of Great Slave Lake some 400 kilometres (250 miles) south of the Arctic Circle, Yellowknife is as colourful as it is cosmopolitan. For every government bureaucrat walking its streets in a suit and tie, there's a miner, prospector, drunk, or raconteur (sometimes all wrapped up in the same body) regaling some newcomer with derring-do stories of gold hunted, fortunes made, loves lost, and blizzards survived. Aboriginals have called the lands around Yellowknife home for thousands of years (the city gets its name from the local Yellowknives Dene peoples, who made tools from copper

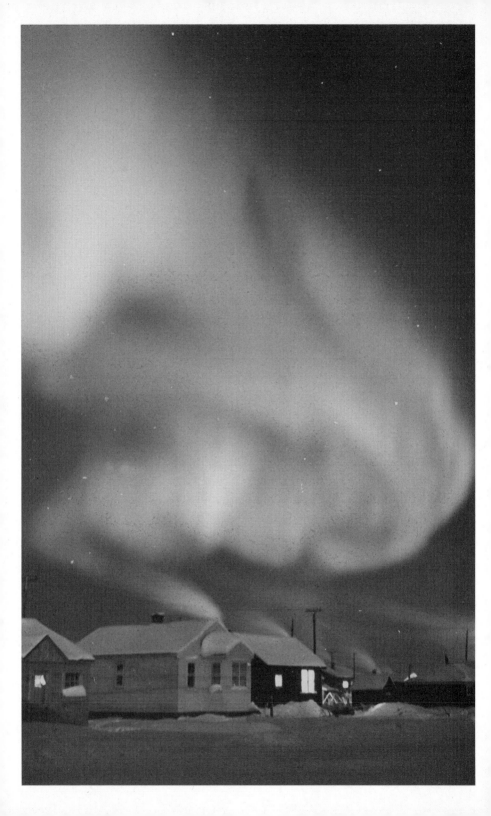

deposits in the area), but the city's modern era began in the 1930s, when gold mining became its primary commercial focus.

The discovery of gold in Yellowknife is widely attributed to a prospector named B.A. Blakeney, who was on his way to the Klondike gold rush around Dawson City, Yukon, in the late 1890s. With the frenzy surrounding the riches being unearthed in the Klondike, people paid little or no attention to Blakeney's Yellowknife discovery. Little wonder: since 1896, when Skookum Jim made his serendipitous discovery of gold along Rabbit (Bonanza) Creek, more than 385,000 kilograms (850,000 pounds) of gold have been taken from the Klondike. There may have been gold around Yellowknife, but nobody seemed to care.

Flying changed the face of prospecting—and of Yellowknife—forever when, in the late 1920s, aircraft were engaged in the search for precious metals across the globe. When uranium and silver were unearthed at Great Bear Lake, about 400 kilometres (250 miles) northwest of Yellowknife, the hunt began in earnest.

In 1933, prospectors Herb Dixon and Johnny Baker found gold in two small lakes near Yellowknife. One year later, gold was found on the east side of Yellowknife Bay, leading to the construction of the Burwash Mine. Though Burwash did not have a particularly long life, the establishment of the mine helped put Yellowknife on the prospecting map. The long-lived Con Mine soon followed. Yellowknife became a full-blown boomtown. Southerners flocked there for both work and adventure.

By 1942, Yellowknife had five gold mines in production. After the lull induced by World War II, the Giant Mine uncovered a significant gold deposit on the north end of town, a discovery that led to yet another staking rush in the

Prospectors braved the ravages of weather and loneliness for a chance at the gold the North was rumoured to hold. Here prospector Curtis Smith searches for the motherlode in the bush around Prairie Creek, Northwest Territories, 1952.

area. Before long, Yellowknife was the economic hub of the Northwest Territories; it was named capital in 1967, the centenary of Canadian confederation.

By the time the 1980s rolled around, Yellowknife's precious-metals era had begun drawing to a close (the last of the gold mines shut its doors in 2004), only to be replaced by an even more desirable product. In 1991, diamonds were discovered a few hundred kilometres north of the city, and the second boom was on. The Ekati Diamond Mine—one of the most prolific on Earth—began operation in 1998. Today, Yellowknife serves as a hub for industry, transportation, communications, education, health, tourism, commerce, and government activity in the territory.

COINCIDENTALLY ENOUGH, my first experience of Yellowknife occurred the same year that diamonds were discovered at Lac de Gras, though profit was the farthest thing from my mind. Eager to carve out my own simple niche in the world, I wanted nothing more than the twenty-dollar weekly stipend Frontiers Foundation afforded me, as long as the organization continued to provide room and board. So after a three-day drive across some of the most remote and unpopulated regions of Canada, I glanced up from the passenger seat of a mid-1970s Chevy Blazer and saw something I never thought I'd see this close to the Arctic Circle: a skyline.

Any urban dweller worth his salt will tell you that Yellowknife's profile is a far cry from New York's. But for me, I'll never forget the moment I laid eyes upon the buildings of the Northwest Territories' capital rising from the frozen subarctic landscape. Three days later I was on a flight bound for Inuvik, itself a four-hour drive from Fort McPherson. As our pickup rumbled down the gravel bed of the Dempster Highway toward our destination, my path became clear: with six months of construction experience under my belt and full of the piss and vinegar of young adulthood, I would meet the North head-on and throw all my energy into my volunteer work. And if that meant pounding nails into the side of a house as outside temperatures dipped low enough to freeze my eyelids shut, so be it.

Yet as fate so often has it, the Arctic had other plans for me.

"You're going to meet your wife up there," one of my Park Avenue colleagues had said to me as I packed up my things and took one last walk around the Major League Baseball office, still wondering if leaving its luxurious confines made any sense.

The odds seemed slim at best. If I hadn't met Mrs. Right from among the eight million or so people who call New York City home, how on Earth would it happen north of the Arctic Circle? The overwhelming majority of Fort McPherson's residents are aboriginal, from families that have hunted, trapped, and fished in the area for generations. Meet my wife? Not unless she was willing to give up a lifestyle that was completely alien to me and spend a little time in the Big Apple.

Yet meet my wife I did. Marty was a nurse in Fort McPherson's small health centre. I remember meeting her on one of the town's dirt roads shortly after my arrival in early January 1991. I was walking down the street with my fellow volunteers, headed back to our small apartment for a bite of lunch after a morning's work. Marty was on a lunchtime stroll with a friend, whose new house we happened to be building.

Though I was smitten with Marty's smile immediately, I had little idea what lurked under the mounds of clothing she wore to ward off the elements. At −40°, we all looked like pears, so one could only speculate whether someone had a nice one of these or impressive set of those. Someone once told me that getting amorous with someone for the first time up north is a bit like opening a Christmas present, except you don't really know how much wrapping paper there is.

Wrapping paper notwithstanding, it wasn't long before Marty and I bid a sad farewell to Fort McPherson and set out on our own adventure together, shuttling from Fort McPherson to

Dozens of small communities pepper the lands that stretch across the 60th parallel. Settled and built almost exclusively by the Canadian government, most of these hamlets boast cookie-cutter homes and a few roads, surrounded by thousands of square kilometres of wilderness.

Indonesia, Hong Kong, Singapore, Thailand, and New York City before returning to the Arctic, this time to the frozen tundra of Baffin Island. A few years later we were married on the sea ice of Patricia Bay near Clyde River, a community of seven hundred-odd Inuit residents. We chose January 21 as our date, the day the sun was set to return to the northern sky (albeit briefly) after a hiatus of more than two months.

After a year in Clyde River we moved southward to the relatively balmy climes of Pangnirtung, another Baffin Island community, but one located about fifty kilometres (thirty miles) south of the Arctic Circle. Our first child, Dawson Orion (named respectively for the Yukon town and the constellation that filled the dark Baffin Island sky all winter), joined our family on March 6, 1996.

Compared with Clyde River, Pangnirtung—or Pang, for short—was a metropolis. The place had two stores, a vibrant arts centre, and even a restaurant, to the extent that a KFC Quickstop counts as a restaurant. Armed with a new work visa and a master's degree in elementary education (that I'd pick up in New York), I took a half-time teaching position in the local junior/senior high school, the Attagoyuk School.

Teaching Grade 9 students at Attagoyuk showed me how little I knew about northern society and culture. Here I was, trying to foist a Canadian-government-approved curriculum upon a group of people who until recently had lived off the land, a tradition they had held for thousands of years. Sure, the kids in my class, with their Montreal Canadiens caps and baggy jeans, looked like a typical group of fourteen-year-olds. But while I was urging them to memorize the parts of speech, they could have been out seal hunting or riding snowmobiles across the frozen waters of Pangnirtung Fiord—a far more enticing prospect. When spring, and nearly constant daylight, came around, attendance in my class plummeted to single digits. The local kids, I learned, had a penchant for staying up all night and sleeping all day.

And while those were simple, carefree days, Dawson's birth forced Marty and me to consider what our future lives would look like. After months of introspection, we realized that Baffin Island—where thousands of kilometres separated us from our families—might not be the ideal place to raise a child.

So when *Up Here* magazine offered me its editorship, I could not refuse. It was an opportunity to take the reins of one of Canada's finest—yet most anonymous—magazines. Published eight times a year, the magazine chronicles the ins and outs of life north of 60, and does so with an eye toward humour, irony, and intrigue. It was, and remains, one of the best reads in the country. Better yet, the offices of *Up Here* were located in Yellowknife, capital of the Northwest Territories and home to around twenty thousand people (good god!). It sure as hell wasn't New York City, but after two years on Baffin Island, it may as well have been.

YELLOWKNIFE HASN'T CHANGED all that much in the years since I last called it home. The city still manages to elegantly blend its frontier history with its cosmopolitan present. Everywhere you look, old and new stand side by side and somehow manage to work together.

The city is perched atop and around the two primary geographic elements that define its boundaries: rocks and water. Frame Lake forms the unofficial centre of town, and many of the city's most significant downtown buildings—City Hall, the Prince of Wales Northern Heritage Centre, and the Northwest

Yellowknife's Old Town strikes an eclectic pose from the air. Like many parts of the city, Old Town has evolved around the outcrops of Canadian Shield that pepper the northern landscape.

Territories Legislative Assembly—share its waterfront views. Jackfish Lake, Niven Lake, Kam Lake, Range Lake, and Rat Lake all add to Yellowknife's watery landscape.

Yet for all the lakeside views the city may offer, it's ultimately the gritty but smooth grey rock that defines the place. No matter where you are in the city, you'll find random outcrops, often in the unlikeliest places. Intrepid developers and homesteaders have tried to tame the rock, blasting it into a more manageable shapes and sizes, but usually the rock prevails, forcing them to come up with unique designs so their domiciles will fit over and around the lichen-flecked stone.

Yellowknife's pioneer roots lie in Old Town, which sits on a small, rocky peninsula jutting out into Yellowknife Bay, a protected arm of Great Slave Lake. For me, this is the city at its most interesting. Turn one way and there's an old, weathered cabin that speaks to decades of hardworking people trying to scratch a living from a land that does not easily yield its secrets or riches. Turn the other to find a modern, funky home designed by a local architect and perched high on a rock, its spacious deck overlooking the lake. Visitors are always delighted by the frontier feel of Old Town's Ragged Ass Road; at some point in the town's colourful history, three local fellows enjoyed some refreshments at the Gold Range Hotel and decided to rename their street as such, erecting a hand-painted sign that very night. Soon afterwards, Ragged Ass Road was adopted as the street's official moniker.

Aptly enough, New Town is the more modern part of Yellowknife; its settlement began after World War ii, when Old Town became overcrowded. Since then, the city has continued to expand outward, and what was once New Town is more commonly regarded as downtown. This is the commercial hub of the city, and where you'll find most of its larger buildings.

From New Town, Yellowknife sprawls. Maybe that's why it sometimes feels more like suburbia than the subarctic city it is. Here you'll find most of Yellowknife's modern-day amenities, such as its pool, recreation facility, and even a Walmart. Most Buffalo employees live in that sprawling—and more affordable— part of town. The McBryans live in Old Town.

As I continued my reacquaintance with Yellowknife in earnest, I realized that despite any cosmetic changes that may have occurred since I left, the heart and soul of the place is the same. A few subdivisions weren't here back then, and some of the buildings had changed shape and purpose, but the heart and soul of Yellowknife was the same. And at its core, Yellowknife is a hard-working, hard-playing, hard-living town. For Buffalo Airways, it's the perfect place to call home.

Pilots' Monument

SITTING atop an eighteen-metre (sixty-foot) hump of rock in Old Town, Pilots' Monument was erected to honour the bush pilots of the 1920s and 1930s who helped open the North to the rest of Canadians. The plaque on the monument reads as follows:

> In the 1920s and 1930s a small number of daring aviators broke the silence of the North. Often flying in extreme cold and facing dangerous takeoff and landing conditions, these bush pilots ferried passengers, mail and freight in and out of remote frontier regions and played a crucial role in the development of the Northern economy and the delivery of public services. Blazing air trails over immense areas, these intrepid pioneers helped map the Canadian Shield and the Arctic Barrenlands, and pilots transformed Northern life by bringing this unique region into the Canadian mainstream.

Mikey McBryan understands well that few other places on Earth could support an airline like Buffalo. From Yellowknife, Buffalo can serve the entire Northwest Territories, all 1.17 million square kilometres (450,000 square miles) of it (not to mention the 2.1 million square kilometres, or 810,000 square miles, of neighbouring Nunavut). There may be only 42,000 people living in the Northwest Territories, but half of them are scattered over a land mass twice the size of Texas. And for many of those people, there's only one way in or out: by air.

Here, on the Earth's last frontier, mavericks are still free to set their own course and dictate their own fate. It's a perfect milieu for someone like Buffalo Joe, who runs his business according to a simple mantra that rings true throughout northern Canada: *get 'er done.*

Yellowknife is the largest and most cosmopolitan city in the Northwest Territories, covering an area of 105.2 square kilometres (40.6 square miles). Actress Margot Kidder, who played Lois Lane in the *Superman* movies, was born here in 1948.

SINCE JOE FOUNDED BUFFALO, the airline has made a name for itself by connecting people living in remote northern communities with the goods they need to live. Up here, the company serves as a lifeline to the North. Take Buffalo out of the picture, and precious food and supplies wouldn't reach the many northern communities that are otherwise cut off from the rest of the world. Although Buffalo delivers freight throughout the year, its effect is most acutely felt during the long, dark winters.

There is no way to characterize a day in the life of Buffalo as "typical." I watched Mikey arrange flights to carry heavy equipment to remote mining camps, deliver massive diesel generators to Inuit communities that rely on them for electricity, ensure a group of bureaucrats would make an early-morning meeting in Whitehorse, and move a single man and his dog to a distant town to start a new life. In other words, if it needs to be moved, Buffalo can move it—and likely already has.

The backbone of Buffalo's winter freight operation is its so-called "valley run," a trip that sees the Curtiss-Wright c-46 fly the 1,700-kilometre (1,056-mile) round trip up and down the Mackenzie River from Yellowknife to four communities that can be accessed only by air nine months of the year: Déline, Tulita, Norman Wells, and Fort Good Hope. Several times each week, the c-46 starts its engines and soars over the valley. And if I was impressed by the DC-3 when I first laid eyes and hands upon her beautifully dimpled frame, I had no idea what lay in store for me when the c-46 was moved into the hangar. It is nothing short of a massive, yawning beast.

THE CURTISS-WRIGHT C-46 COMMANDO made a splash when it was introduced to the world at the 1939 New York World's Fair. It was heralded as the latest and greatest in high-altitude pressurized aircraft, ready for the enjoyment of the flying public.

The plane was not formally released until two years later, just as World War II was taking over the global stage. The designers of the c-46 may have envisioned it as a glamorous passenger airplane, but fate turned it into a bare-knuckled military aircraft. Instead of carrying passengers to the far corners of the globe, the c-46 played host to war supplies, paratroopers, ammunition, artillery, and wounded soldiers.

A total of 1,430 c-46s were built, a far cry from the more than 10,000 DC-3s that dominated the skies during the war.

C-46 Facts & Figures

- CAPACITY: 4 flight crew and 62 passengers
- PRODUCTION: 1,430
- LENGTH: 23.3 metres (76 feet, 4 inches)
- WINGSPAN: 32.9 metres (108 feet, 1 inch)
- HEIGHT: 6.6 metres (21 feet, 9 inches)
- MAXIMUM SPEED: 433 km/h (269 MPH)
- CRUISE SPEED: 278 km/h (173 MPH)
- RANGE: 4,750 kilometres (2,950 miles)
- EMPTY WEIGHT: 14,700 kilograms (32,400 pounds)
- MAXIMUM TAKEOFF WEIGHT: 21,800 kilograms (48,000 pounds)

But the C-46 offered benefits that the DC-3 couldn't even touch. Known by a variety of nicknames to the flyboys who manned her controls in both the European and Pacific theatres (she was called the "Killer Whale," the "Curtiss Calamity," the "T-Cat," or "Dumbo," after the flying elephant she resembles), the Commando could fly at high altitude and carry massive payloads, two of its most important traits.

The twin-engine C-46 was helped by the addition of its power plants, the newly invented 18-cylinder Pratt & Whitney R-2800, each of which delivered 2,000 horsepower. They were so powerful that they could keep a lightly loaded C-46 in the air even if one engine failed, an attractive characteristic at a time when bullets were routinely screaming through the skies. When both engines were firing, the plane could carry as much as fifteen thousand pounds of cargo.

Though the 46 made its presence known throughout the war, it was perhaps best known for its role in the China-Burma-India theatre, where it carried supplies over the jagged peaks of the Himalayas from India and Burma to troops fighting in

Here they come —
the **CURTISS-COMMANDOS!**

"Swarming down from the skies, Allied gliders and parachute troops captured enemy airfields . . ." More and more in the day's news, words such as these reveal the vital part that transport and cargo planes are playing in the swift invasion of enemy-held areas.

The Curtiss-Commando, the world's largest twin-engined transport, has a leading role in this new and revolutionary phase of the war. These giants of the air telescope weeks into hours and perform prodigies in swift movements of men and materiel.

CURTISS-WRIGHT
Corporation
AIRPLANE DIVISION

FIRST
Since the Birth of Aviation

1920 · Curtiss Eagle, first inter-city "liner," 400 h.p., 10 passengers, 105 m.p.h.–64' wing span.

1929 · Curtiss B-2 Condor Bomber for the U.S. Army. Greatest weight carrying airplane of its time. Heavy defensive armament. Two Curtiss Conqueror engines.

1929 · Curtiss Condor, 2 pilots and 18 passengers, 139 m.p.h. high speed, two 600 h.p. Curtiss Conqueror engines.

1933 · Curtiss Condor, the first sleeper plane—8 compartments, each with 2 berths, two 720 h.p. Wright Cyclone engines, 167 m.p.h. cruising.

The Curtiss-Wright C-46 Commando played a significant role in the U.S. military's World War II efforts in Europe and Asia, and the company was quick to inform the public of its successes in these theatres. After the war, the CIA became an avid user of the plane.

China. The c-46 wasn't the only plane to serve this role, but it was certainly the best.

After World War II ended, military service continued for the 46, essentially dooming its potential as a passenger aircraft. Its presence was still felt around the globe, though in far more covert ways. The CIA used the plane to support French forces fighting communist insurgencies in French Indochinese countries such as Vietnam, Cambodia, and Laos, and in Thailand. The 46 also played a part in clandestine anti-communist campaigns of the late 1940s and early 1950s, such as supplying Chiang Kai-shek's troops while they battled Mao's Communists. In 1961, the c-46 operated in the Bay of Pigs Invasion. The planes even served in the early years of the Vietnam War before being officially retired from active combat duty in 1968.

Life for the c-46 did not stop there. The aircraft's rapid climb rate and high service ceiling made it ideal for flying over the Andes in countries such as Bolivia, Peru, Argentina, and Chile. It easily covered vast stretches of South American jungle where roads did not exist. Today, a handful of c-46s are still in use throughout the world, transporting goods to otherwise inaccessible regions from Alaska to Kenya.

Buffalo Joe likes the c-46 because the aluminum alloy aircraft is virtually indestructible and can take off and land on small airstrips, making it the ideal candidate for the valley run. The way Joe sees it, the c-46 must be a great plane if it's still working regularly around the world. As he says, a lot of planes have come and gone since then. Rod McBryan, director of maintenance at Buffalo and Joe's eldest son, agrees. As Rod says, given the weather conditions in the north, the 46 is the only logical choice to be running tons of goods up and down the Mackenzie Valley.

Despite its rich history and legendary status in the aviation world, the c-46 is hampered by one significant drawback: it's a bitch to fly. With its wide fuselage, broad tail, and small rudder, the c-46 is extremely vulnerable to crosswinds and is only rated to land in a twenty-two-kilometre-an-hour (fourteen-mile-per-hour) crosswind. Compounding the issue is the fact that most of the aircraft's weight is located behind the main wheels, which means the back end can swing around if the plane's not landed straight. And as Buffalo's former chief pilot Arnie Schreder says, a c-46 tail that starts to swing on landing will continue to swing on landing. "If you look around the Arctic, there are c-46s strewn all over it," he says. "And those crashes were always due to wind."

If the secret to an airline's success with the c-46 is expert pilots, then Buffalo has nothing to worry about. The 46 may be the toughest plane in the Buffalo fleet to fly, but Joe's system of separating the wheat from the chaff among his young pilots means that only the brightest, most competent, and hardest-working pilots get to sit at the controls of that massive bird, and only after they've paid their dues on smaller, easier-to-fly craft like the DC-3.

That fact holds true for all but one member of the Buffalo team. At six-feet-seven, Scott Blue is simply too big to fit behind the controls of the DC-3. He can squeeze himself in there tightly enough, cross his legs, and cruise. But control the ailerons (the small, hinged "winglets" attached to the trailing edges of the wings) and rudder pedals with his feet and try to bring it down safely in a crosswind? Not happening. So Joe and Scott had no choice: Scott earned his stripes on the c-46.

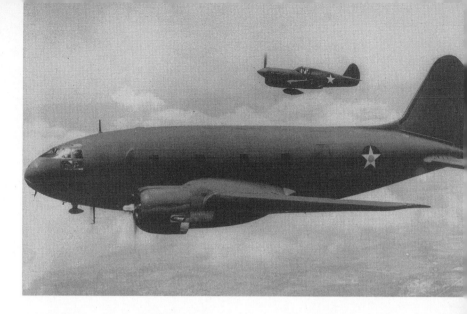

The "Dumbo" was an imposing figure in the skies over World War II battle-fields. Here the c-46 flies in tandem with the Curtiss p-40 Warhawk, one of the most famous fighter planes used during the war.

"I love the 46 because you can never take it for granted," Blue says. "It'll kick your ass, no matter how good a pilot you are." Even captains who have flown the c-46 for thousands of hours will tell you the plane stubbornly refuses to be mastered.

"A.J. [Decoste] is one of the best drivers I know, and even he has some days where a landing doesn't go as well as he wanted," Blue says. "And that man knows that plane cold. He is an amazing driver! And even he has days where he just can't figure it out. It's an amazing machine in terms of what it can do, but you really have to know what you're doing to drive it properly. You've got to treat it with a whole lot of respect."

IF ANY MEMBER of the Buffalo crew can speak to the challenges—and joys—of flying the c-46, it's Jeff Schroeder, a senior pilot who's been flying the plane for more than twenty years.

The first time I met Jeff, we were in the Buffalo hangar standing beside the mammoth airplane. You wouldn't necessarily think that a guy who has sat at the controls of the 46 for more than twenty-four years and twenty thousand hours—likely making him the most experienced c-46 captain in the universe—would find his job exciting. But as he began to talk about the plane, his enthusiasm became palpable. Here's a guy who literally shakes when he describes what it feels like to sit in the left seat of one of the most exotic planes on the planet.

"People always say if you love something, you'd do it for free," the Winnipeg resident told me with a huge grin on his face.

To the novice eye, the cockpits of Buffalo's vintage aircraft are a dizzying array of knobs, levels, dials, and gauges. Laminated checklists are clipped to the pilot's and co-pilot's yokes.

"Well, it's pretty close to that for me with the 46. There's nothing that sounds like it on takeoff. When it rumbles, it makes so much noise you think it's gonna frickin' explode... it's exciting." No doubt. Just listening to the guy talk gave me goosebumps. He became more and more animated with every word. His hands waved in the air, and his voice took on the distinctive growl of a child making rumbling noises as he pushes a dump truck around a sandbox. "And when the temperature hits thirty below, it cracks and moans. You would swear this thing is just gonna explode. It's buzzing, the props are buzzing, and it's shaking and it's rattling.

"You know," he brought his arms back to his sides and caught his breath, "it's been twenty-four years for me, and I still get excited talking about the thing. It's a thrill ride every time, it really is."

When Jeff was checked out on the 46 for Air Manitoba, in 1986, he was that company's last pilot to receive his captaincy on the Dumbo. At the time, few of his colleagues could figure out why someone would want to waste his time on a flying dinosaur.

"I said 'You know what, I don't see the 46 ever going out of business, other than a shortage of parts or something like that,'" he told me, the grin on his face stubbornly refusing to dissipate. "Let's face it, what else can haul fourteen thousand pounds as cheaply as the c-46 does? There's nothing else out there—to this day—that can do it." As Mikey says, the c-46 is a rarity in the aircraft industry: it can pay itself off in a month.

For Jeff, sticking with a plane that everyone else thought was destined for the scrapheap meant a lot of job security. "I just knew there was a future there, and stuck it out while the other guys went other places. And for the last twenty-four years, I haven't had to deal with the airlines or layoffs, or work shortages—nothing like that. I guess if you're good at what you do, there's always work, eh?"

Jeff doesn't live in Yellowknife, choosing instead to commute from his home in Winnipeg and stay in Yellowknife for stints ranging anywhere from two to eight weeks, depending on Joe's needs. But since Jeff's other occasional employer—First Nations Transportation—went out of business in 2009, his Buffalo flying is taking on even greater importance.

The way Jeff tells it, the Dumbo is the most difficult plane in the world to fly. "Three-quarters of all the c-46s ever built have been destroyed on takeoff or landing," Jeff related matter-of-factly. "That's when the pilot's ability has to shine."

Jeff's ability has had that chance on more occasions than he cares to remember. Take, for example, the time Buffalo took on a job that would see the 46 shuttle a huge backlog of cargo from Thompson, Manitoba, bound for the remote community of St. Theresa Point, an hour's flight southeast of Thompson. Typically, St. Theresa Point residents receive their winter deliveries via trucks that travel the ice road, but this particular year, the ice roads were in such bad shape that the trucks couldn't get through.

Shortly after takeoff on one leg of the job, the left engine began making a horrific noise. To Jeff's chagrin, the engine began leaking oil shortly thereafter. With the plane loaded to capacity, Jeff had little choice but to get her on the ground—fast.

With the engine sounding worse and worse every second, Jeff had a split-second decision to make. Should he turn around and try to make it back to Thompson, or look for an alternative? Luckily, he remembered that the tiny community of Island Lake—population fifty-nine—had a gravel airstrip, where he was able to bring the 46 down before disaster struck.

As Buffalo pilots know all too well, their job does not begin and end in the cockpit. To be a Buffalo pilot is to be resourceful. If there was ever a professional who had to mimic the 1980s television star MacGyver—the secret agent who could craft a neutron bomb out of a Swiss Army knife and some old cheese— it's the Buffalo Airways pilot. So Jeff, Scott, and flight engineer James Dwojak pulled the oil screen off the engine and began their investigation.

The aluminum shards and flakes waiting for them were a telltale sign of a broken cylinder. When a cylinder breaks, the piston grinds against the cylinder wall, shredding bits of metal along the way. The only thing to do was remove the cylinder, a job that proved easier said than done.

Unable to wedge the stubborn cylinder out of the engine with their own muscle, the trio then turned to their ingenuity. They ran a couple of heavy-duty ratcheting nylon straps (often called "herc straps") from the cylinder to the back of a pickup truck, then revved up the truck. The cylinder didn't budge. The crew had no choice but to call in reinforcements with a replacement engine. Then they hitched a ride back to Thompson with a twenty-four-year-old New Zealand woman who runs a small air taxi service out of Island Lake.

For most of us, that kind of adventure is a never-in-a-lifetime thing. Here are two men buzzing around in a fully loaded plane that very likely ferried troops during World War II, and one of its engine blows. Put me in the cockpit and the result would be nothing short of a myocardial infarction. For the Buffalo boys? No problem. Just get 'er down and get 'er fixed.

It's just another day at the wackiest airline on Earth.

4

THE FAMILY BUSINESS

Upon further reflection, "wacky" may be a strong word to describe Buffalo Airways. Sure, day-to-day life there can be, er, *unique*, but the foundation upon which Buffalo operates is as simple and straightforward as it comes.

Indeed, from the "rampies" struggling on the frozen tarmac of the Yellowknife and Hay River airports—hoping one day to defy the odds, crack the upper echelon of the Buffalo hierarchy, and actually get behind the controls of a piece of flying history—to the people slogging away in the company's cargo headquarters just down the street from the hangar, life at Buffalo Airways is work, work, work.

And it doesn't matter if you're related to the boss. If anything, Mikey, his sister Kathy (who manages the Hay River operation), and brother Rod (the company's director of maintenance) are held to an even higher standard. Rod's perspective on work/life balance changed with the birth of his first child—daughter Emma Rae was born on May 8, 2010—but Mikey is unrepentantly single. And right now the most important relationship in his life is with his job. In fact, when I met him for the first time, Mikey told me that he hadn't had a day off while in Yellowknife for over a year. If he's in town, he's working. If he needs a day off, he has to go away. "I don't work at Buffalo Airways," Mikey said, "I *live* at Buffalo Airways."

Although there is no such thing as a typical day in the life of Mikey McBryan—managing a small airline in one of the harshest climates on Earth will keep you on your toes—he is usually at work by 7:30 every morning (often earlier) to get ready for the arrival of the sked (airline lingo for a plane that's part of a scheduled service) from Hay River. From then on it's a whirlwind of activity that includes anything you could imagine: quoting jobs to prospective clients, flying to distant countries to buy long-forgotten and disused planes that could be coaxed back to life at the hands of Buffalo mechanics, managing the company's ever-growing public image (a task he's particularly fond of), or designing another round of T-shirts to sell at his now wildly successful Buffalo Airwear Internet store. Like his dad, Mikey finds little time to rest.

It's hard to imagine Mikey dedicating himself as much to his work as his father does, but there's certainly enough on his plate to keep him consumed 24/7. Buffalo employs seventy to eighty full-time employees, whom Mikey calls the "hard-core employees." Then there's another twenty-odd people who work for the company on a contract-by-contract basis, usually

Ice Roads—Not Just for Truckers

CONTRARY to popular belief, ice roads are not just for truckers. In fact, they are used by polar dwellers all over the world, from Estonia to Finland, Canada to Russia. At first blush, ice roads are little more than pathways scraped across frozen bays, rivers, lakes, and seas. They allow temporary access to otherwise inaccessible areas and towns. Ice roads are commonly found where the construction of a permanent road is cost prohibitive, typically across the boggy muskeg of the northern tundra.

Driving across an ice road is a fairly clear-cut undertaking, since the roads are usually straight, with few obstacles. Of course, driving over open water always presents an element of danger, especially when loads get heavy, as with transport trucks. Heavier vehicles need to limit their speed on the ice road to approximately twenty-five kilometres (fifteen miles) an hour or they create waves under the surface of the water, which can either damage the road or dislodge the ice from the shoreline.

In Canada, John Denison is considered the father of the ice road, having engineered several of the earliest ones in the 1950s and 1960s, including one between Yellowknife and the Eldorado Mine at Port Radium on the eastern shore of Great Bear Lake, some 450 kilometres (280 miles) to the north.

pilots who come in for a week or two at a time, or who special-ize in certain aircraft.

It's not as though Buffalo has a lock on northern cargo transport, either. Sure, the company is one of the biggest players in the northern game, but Mikey knows that First Air, a passenger and charter airline based in Ottawa, is always breathing down his neck with its two Yellowknife-based Lockheed c-130 Hercules aircraft. "And the only way we know how much they compete with us is because we get so much busier when they have a plane down," Mikey told me. "That's how you know your competition."

If Mikey is the least bit leery of his rivals stealing some of his business, he certainly doesn't show it. "We all technically do the same thing: we go into communities with no roads. I guess the difference is these other companies are basically passenger airlines, while we're primarily a cargo company."

Yet as so many people—both in the Canadian North and around the world—have come to know, Buffalo is much more than just an air cargo company. The simple fact that there are very few airlines on *Earth* that can claim a unique fleet such as this is testimony enough to the company's place in the pantheon of modern-day air travel. As Mikey says, while there are other airlines around the world that fly a few of these old warbirds (Alaska's Everts Air Cargo and Colombia's Saldeca are two), none can claim such an extensive fleet of flying history.

With so many things to look after, it's no wonder that Mikey's work day continues long after he's left the confines of Buffaloworld. Whenever we go to lunch, Mikey's phone rings every few minutes. And when his phone's not ringing, he's constantly sending and receiving texts and emails, hundreds per day. On one frozen February afternoon, Mikey and I are sitting opposite each other at his favourite Yellowknife haunt, Surly Bob's sports bar. (Mikey also has a soft spot for the local strip club, Harley's Hard Rock Saloon, particularly on Monday evenings, when a new stripper arrives from Edmonton for a week-long stint in the Knife). We're not looking at each other, though, as our heads are buried deep in our iPhones. "You know," Surly Bob growls as he hands us our meals, "you could just look at each other and *talk*."

As if. Mikey gets fifty to sixty-five calls on a slow day, a hundred if things are getting hot and heavy. The guy goes through a new cellphone about every four months and is an expert on cellphone technology.

Like so many people his age—he was born in 1982, when I was making my way through high school—Mikey is more comfortable with technology than he is without it. He doesn't seem to care all that much about what he wears, what he drives (a beat-up 1989 Buffalo Airways Ford Ranger), or the condition of his house, which seems to be in a state of perpetual renovation and/or repair. But when it comes to technology, Mikey is dialled in.

The focal point of Mikey's living room is a massive sixty-two-inch flat-screen TV. When he's not at work, he spends a fair bit of time in front of it, simultaneously watching and working on his MacBook Pro. Sure, he's got his satellite TV, Blu-ray player, and other digital accoutrements that adorn the living rooms of most North American families these days. But what separates Mikey from the rest of us mere viewers is that Mikey is a *student* of technology. He is addicted to social networking and thinks that Facebook may be the greatest innovation since the Ski-Doo.

"I can probably attribute thirty thousand dollars a year in merchandise sales directly to Facebook," he told me one evening as we relaxed in his living room. "So how can I not be fully behind that kind of technology?"

Yet as much as it may have profited him, Mikey also appreciates Facebook for its ability to thrust its users—*all* of its users—into the global spotlight. "Sure, the people who are private will always be private," he says. "But I think people tend to be narcissistic; that's human nature. So thanks to Facebook, everybody is a celebrity now."

Admittedly, some of us achieve greater celebrity than others, regardless of the Facebook phenomenon. *I* don't have people throwing themselves all over me in distant airports. *I* don't have strange women texting me photos of their scantily clad and/or unclad bodies. And *I* don't have business owners from all over the globe sending me cases of their wares, in the hopes that I may eat it, use it, mention it, or wear it on my wildly successful TV show. Mikey does.

As I reflect on his celebrity—and the phenomenon that *Ice Pilots* has become—I begin to realize just how much foresight, intelligence, creativity, and business acumen this frat-boy-cum-TV-star possesses.

AS YOU MIGHT EXPECT, Mikey's indoctrination into the world of aviation did not start at adulthood. Buffalo Airways has been a constant in his life for as long as he can remember.

He was born and raised in Hay River, Northwest Territories, a town of slightly more than thirty-five hundred people perched just north of the 60th parallel. The town sits where the Hay River empties into Great Slave Lake, and has built a reputation as a transportation hub for the rest of the Northwest Territories (it calls itself "The Hub of the North"). This is largely due to the fact that Hay River is the northernmost point in North America connected to the continental railway system. Hay River is also a major staging point for the many barges that ply the waters of the Mackenzie River during the summer, when northern communities along the river stock their larders as much as possible before winter sets in.

Until 1968, when the highway to Yellowknife was built, Hay River was literally the end of the road, which made the town the ideal place to run an airline. Yellowknife may be the home of Buffalo's massive hangar, and the site of all of its northern-based maintenance, but Hay River is the company's legal base of operations.

"I was always in the hangar," Mikey told me. "I was honestly—legitimately—raised by rampies." He was a snot-nosed kid, always lurking around the hangar, constantly underfoot. He would be passed off from rampie to rampie, and he would drive around in courier vans with them each day. They even took young Mikey on fishing and ATV trips. "So I really was raised by them."

Buffalo started its twice-daily Hay River–Yellowknife passenger service the year Mikey was born, so Joe was not a constant figure in his son's life when Mikey was growing up in Hay River. "Every day he was gone to Yellowknife and wouldn't come back until later that night. That's all I've ever known," Mikey said as we waited in the hangar one morning for the sked to arrive from Hay River.

"Hey," I asked as the DC-3 touched down in front of us with the yelp of rubber hitting asphalt, "is your Dad gonna greet you with a big hug and kiss? Tell you how much he loves you?"

"More like he'll tell me about something I've screwed up," Mikey said with a laugh. He understands how his father operates, and if there's any resentment corked up inside Mikey's body, he does a hell of a good job covering it up. To the contrary, while Mikey may spend a fair bit of time griping about the old man, I know he admires his dad. "He's not motivated by money at all," said Mikey. "He's motivated by one thing: doing the job. He's completely customer oriented."

In a land where unique personalities are the rule rather than the exception, Joe is in a class of his own. His slicked-back pompadour speaks to his affinity for the 1950s, when he was an adolescent. This man is the product of a bygone era, and one that Mikey says he never quite left. In fact, Mikey considers his dad a cross between Howard Hughes, James Dean, and *Married with Children*'s Al Bundy. "Of the six billion people on Earth, there's nobody else who could run Buffalo," Mikey said.

That may be a bit of a stretch, but Joe is perfectly suited to helm the company. He is stubborn to the point of being unyielding, a trait that helps him keep his commitments to his clients. He is unconventional and uses any means necessary to deliver cargo across vast tracts of untamed wilderness. When your fleet is largely composed of World War II–era planes, thinking outside the box is an important characteristic.

And perhaps most of all, Joe McBryan is simple. Not simple-minded, but rather there is nothing fancy about this man. In all the time I spent in the hangar, I knew I could count on Joe to bring his lunch to work every day, whether it was a bologna sandwich or a plastic container containing leftovers from last night's dinner. Jeans and a plaid work shirt—that's Joe McBryan.

The way Mikey sees it, Joe has created a universe for himself, one that insulates him from the outside world. "He's created himself this world that he can live in so he doesn't have to go outside, really. He lives completely and eccentrically in his own world.

"He's never grown up, because he's never had to," Mikey added. "The moment he became his own boss, he made his own rules."

"This whole thing," he said, waving his arm to indicate the hangar, "is like Disneyland for Joe. It's all his design."

And yet, as Lone Ranger as Joe may seem, the success of Buffalo rests on the fact that the McBryans—all of the McBryans—play an integral role in running the airline, despite their seemingly vast personality and skill differences. "With most family businesses," Mikey said, "everyone's a welder or everyone's a mechanic or everyone's a fisherman. But with us, it's different. My dad's the only pilot, my brother's the mechanic, my sister's the people person, and my mom's the accountant. So we all have our strengths and weaknesses, but we're all so different. It's almost like we're not even family at all."

Though these differences may make for unusual moments around the Thanksgiving table, the McBryans have managed to blend their differences into a fairly tasty stew. Together they make sense. Take one piece out, though, and the result is incomplete. "We can't do each other's job at all, and yet we all can't not work together," Mikey said. "We all need each other for the whole thing to work." In other words, Joe may not need Mikey to fly a plane, but Joe needs Mikey in order to fly the planes. It's an arrangement that works well for the people of the North.

Mikey struggles to identify exactly what his role is (I think "New Media Visionary" has a nice ring to it), even though the TV show calls him general manager. Either way, he has no problem saying what he *isn't*. "I started as a pilot, and didn't do too good. Then I tried to be a mechanic, and didn't do good at all. Then I went into metalwork, but I wasn't very good at that, either. That's when I went to business school, I finally figured out what I'm good at."

When someone in the office up and quit and Joe needed a replacement to work up charter quotes, Mikey was handed the job.

"Essentially it was because nobody else would do it; everyone else was busy fixing and flying the airplanes," he told me.

Not that Mikey needs to feel bad about anything on the work front. As far as I can tell, he has been the driving, on-the-ground force that has changed Buffalo Airways from a business to a worldwide phenomenon. *Ice Pilots,* of course, is the foundation of that genesis.

AFTER GRADUATING from high school, Mikey went to business school at Red Deer College in Red Deer, Alberta, a city of some 100,000 people about halfway between Calgary and Edmonton. Going to school in Red Deer was a no-brainer for him, given his close ties to the city. Buffalo maintains a hangar in nearby Penhold, which allowed Mikey to go away without really going away. "I was still under the umbrella," he told me. "I was still in the Buffalo bubble."

Bubble or not, being away from the daily grind in Hay River and Yellowknife afforded Mikey an opportunity to focus on his business education, though the demographics of his school sometimes made it hard to stay focused. "We Hay River guys, we're not the best-looking guys and all. But Red Deer College had four girls for every guy, because it was all nursing and business students. So we all had the hottest girlfriends!"

One afternoon during his third year there, Mikey was sitting in a marketing class when he received a call from David Gullason, an executive producer at Vancouver-based Omni Film Productions. After introducing himself, David explained that he had recently read an article about Mikey and Buffalo Airways in *The Globe and Mail.*

"David asked me if I wanted to be on television," Mikey said. "I said 'Yeah!'"

"I had read about British tourists—they call them 'propheads'—going to Yellowknife to see these old planes," Gullason told me over the phone one day. "We were looking for an in-the-moment show that had elements of history and science, and this had both. And obviously there was this huge, great unfolding story. What could be better? The planes, the Arctic, and the people who fly them."

IMAGINE YOURSELF WORKING at Buffalo Airways in spring 2008. You're trucking along, doing your job every day in blissful anonymity, trying to survive the unpredictable rigours of the cold, the dark, and Joe's temper. You think you've got it all worked out. Sure, you're working your ass off and sometimes Joe tears you a new rectum, but the place feels like home, the characters like family. Life reaches a comfortable stasis.

Then, without warning, a couple of strangers show up, one of whom is carrying a serious-looking video camera. You're told that your work life is now going to be immortalized on film and broadcast to millions of people in Canada and around the world. And (this is a big *and*) every move you make, every word you say, every screw-up you commit—large or small—is going to be documented, logged, and potentially made the focus of a TV show episode. How would you feel?

Mikey McBryan's Top 10 TV Shows

1 *The Simpsons*
2 *Trailer Park Boys*
3 *Penn & Teller: Bullshit!*
4 *Monster Garage*
5 *Sons of Anarchy*
6 *Family Guy*
7 *Darkwing Duck*
8 *Teenage Mutant Ninja Turtles*
9 *Mr. Dressup*
10 *Ice Pilots NWT*

If you answered "really friggin' uncomfortable," you're not alone. And chances are, you probably would have made your discomfort known to the strangers now skulking around the hangar, sticking a camera in your face at the most inopportune moments and asking you pointed questions about your life and your work.

That is where I found myself in January 2011, when I walked into the alien world of Buffalo Airways, immersed myself in its daily rhythms, and shared the triumph and defeats of the people who work there. Sure, I had faith in my abilities. I had always managed to make people comfortable enough to share the most intimate aspects of their lives with me. But I knew that gaining people's confidence, trust, and friendship would not come right away.

In those early days, I hung around—a lot. People looked at me suspiciously, wondering what the hell I was doing in their lives. Either they wouldn't talk to me, or they simply offered blunt, unemotional responses. Sometimes (though thankfully rarely) they were downright hostile. I felt like an outsider because, frankly, I *was* an outsider. Sure, I had Mikey to act as my buffer, but I still felt the stares, heard the questions. As Joe so bluntly put it at our first meeting: "Book—what book?"

Eventually, I managed to make progress with even the most leery Buffalo employees, but Joe was staunchly resistant to the idea that I even existed. Usually when I asked him a question he grumbled something as he hurried to another part of the hangar. Sometimes his responses were accompanied by a glare that would melt Yellowknife permafrost.

One time I gauged Joe incorrectly, fooling myself into thinking he was in a talkative mood, and asked him about the airline's genesis, hoping for some historical context. "You gotta know this shit," he scowled. "All you gotta do is go on the computer, Google it, and then you get all that information and write that shit up."

"I just think the book could use a bit of historical context, so I was wonderi—"

"Well, if you're writing an article on *Ice Pilots,* I'd be very careful about getting into too much detail. Number one, I ain't gonna do an autobiography. And number two, I ain't gonna do a history of Buffalo Airways."

It helped my ego to know that the TV crew had found itself in the same boat just a couple of years earlier; ever suspicious, Joe wanted nothing to do with them. He would say things like "I don't know why you guys are following me around—this is Mikey's movie."

Joe's ire over the show—and the intrusion into his personal and business life—only grew when he heard the name proposed by the TV production company. "Honestly," Mikey told me conspiratorially, "we all hate the name *Ice Pilots.* It's the worst name ever."

But Mikey understands the logic behind the moniker. As he tells it, the producers wanted the name to max out at eighteen letters, so the entire title could fit on a satellite TV guide. It couldn't be called Buffalo Airways, for fear it would be confused with the city in New York. "As much as we hate it, *Ice Pilots NWT* is a grammatically perfect name," Mikey explained. The word "*Ice*" not only connotes the frigid environment well enough, it also taps into the success of another successful Yellowknife-based reality TV show, *Ice Road Truckers*. "*Pilots*" is self-explanatory enough, while "*NWT*" hints at the remote geography of the place.

The logic was lost on Joe, however. "When my father heard *Ice Pilots,* he wanted nothing to do with the show." The reason Joe hated it, strangely enough, all hinged on the word "*Pilots*." He is an ardent believer that his company's success is about everyone who works for Buffalo, not just the pilots. From the rampies who deliver courier packages in −40° temperatures to the mechanics who dig elbow-deep in oil and muck every day, Joe knows that every piece of the Buffalo puzzle is as vital as the next. "It really hurt him that they named the show *Ice Pilots*," Rod McBryan explained. "Because only about a third of our employees are pilots. What about everyone else?"

Joe was likely also reluctant to reveal insider secrets in one of the most highly regulated industries in the world. But two and a half years later, the *Ice Pilots* and Buffalo Airways crews are one big happy family. The crew now melt into the background of the day-to-day operations of the airline, and they boast strong friendships with the pilots, mechanics, and other staff members who call Buffalo home. I couldn't help but look on with envy as I sometimes crossed paths with Joe and a director or cameraman engaged in friendly conversation.

The Quest for the Perfect Shot

MICHAEL BODNARCHUK has worked as both a director and videographer on *Ice Pilots,* and knows well the dangers of working around powerful machines and getting lost in the moment. On one occasion, Michael was filming a plane readying for taxi and takeoff outside the Buffalo hangar. "It's fairly normal stock footage that we get," he told me. "You get the engines starting, the pilots looking out the window, that sort of thing."

On this day, however, one of the engines wouldn't start, sending co-pilot Scott Blue to fetch a generator to help power up the sluggish engine while the other roared away.

"Scott comes back, walks around the back of the plane and plugs in the generator," Michael said. "And without thinking I just ran under the plane to the left side, got my close-up of him doing his thing, and then retraced my steps and went back to where I was.

"And it wasn't until I got back to where I was standing before that it dawned on me: for an instant I had entertained the notion of walking diagonally to get a cockpit shot. And if I had done that, I would have walked right through the propeller. I've never forgotten that moment, and I won't ever go near a propeller again."

5

RAMPIES

It is said that there are two kinds of people living in the North: those who are running from something and those who can't fit in with the rest of society. After coming to experience life at Buffalo Airways, I would add one more group to that: people who want to become pilots—a.k.a. the "rampies."

Of all the unique, exciting, and somewhat bizarre things I learned during my time with the Buffalo family, nothing would resonate with me quite as much as the rampies. For the uninitiated, rampies are aspiring pilots—usually, but not exclusively, men—who start their flying careers by working on the "ramp," that amorphous area on the tarmac just outside the hangar or terminal where planes are loaded and unloaded at all hours of the day or night, regardless of weather, temperature, or working conditions. Those curmudgeons who hold steadfastly to the notion that "kids today" don't know how to work or are only interested in video games and other narcissistic pursuits haven't been to The Ramp.

And while paying one's dues as a rampie is a fact of life for aspiring pilots the world over, nowhere is it quite so demanding as in the world of Buffalo Airways. I know, because I was one.

OKAY, SAYING I was a rampie is a *bit* of a stretch, since my time as a member of the Brotherhood of the Ramp comprises, well, not a hell of a lot. But it didn't take long for me to see that the old-school work ethic that so many people yearn for in today's youth is alive and well.

It was −25°C (−13°F) the first morning I showed up to the ramp, and the wind was screaming across the darkened runway of the Yellowknife airport. I wasn't sure what the day would hold, so I was woefully unprepared for the work to come. I left my snow pants in the warm confines of my new home away from home, Birches B & B, the same place I left my Canadian Army arctic survival boots. And even thought I had my down parka, heavy mitts, and rabbit-fur trapper's hat, the icy fingers of the wind managed to pick their way through every microscopic nook and cranny my clothing offered—*every* nook and cranny.

It was 8:00 AM, and we rampies were anxiously awaiting the arrival of a freighter DC-3 from Hay River. The Hay River–Yellowknife route is just one of many cargo routes that Buffalo flies, but it's a critical one. Every night, a Buffalo Air Express transport truck drives from Edmonton to Hay River, about one thousand kilometres (620 miles) to the north, loaded with goods and documents bound for various communities across the Northwest Territories and Nunavut.

On some days there's not much cargo to be hauled, and it fits on the sked that Joe flies up from Hay River every morning. Other mornings see heavier loads, and an empty DC-3 or DC-4 needs to be flown down to Hay River at six in the morning to pick up the goods and bring them back to Yellowknife. My guide for this day was Laurent Dussault, a French Canadian from Montreal who goes by the nickname "French Larry."

Once the plane taxied to the hangar, the work began in earnest. A half dozen Buffalo Airways vans lined up near the plane's cargo doors, engines running in the bitter cold of early morning. (Running engines are a fact of life in a Yellowknife winter. On −40° days, so many cars are kept running in the city that the streets are filled with ice fog from vehicle exhaust.) Soon the load was being unstrapped from the plane's interior, and the work hit a breakneck pace. As the various boxes, crates, and envelopes made their way out, their destination was shouted and the package moved to the appropriate van. Despite the commotion, I couldn't help noticing a man I hadn't met before, one who intrigued me with his dark and heavily creased face, and the gap-toothed smile that never seemed to stop flashing.

Jimmy Essery—a.k.a. "the Indian"—is one of those guys who rarely gets any *Ice Pilots* screen time but is an integral part of Buffalo. An on-and-off presence at the Yellowknife hangar since 1986, Jimmy epitomizes what the North and the airline are all about: he works hard—and lives harder.

Ask Jimmy what he does, and the answer comes quickly: "I do everything. Whatever it takes to make Buffalo work." Doesn't matter if it's servicing the aircraft, mopping hangar floors, or building an ice strip in the middle of nowhere, Jimmy has been there. Maybe that's why I could always count on finding Jimmy in the hangar, whether it was four in the morning or ten at night.

Originally from outside Hearst, Ontario, Jimmy arrived in Yellowknife on April Fool's Day, 1970, just a few weeks before Joe started Buffalo Airways in Hay River. It didn't take long for Jimmy to settle into his favourite Yellowknife haunts. "I wasn't old enough to go to the bar, but I still did."

From what other people tell me, Jimmy's relationship with Buffalo is a strange on-again, off-again phenomenon. When he's there, he's *there*. Then he'll just disappear for a while. "I make up my own hours. If I feel like I'm doggin' it and not producing, I just wander off and come when it's busy."

You get the feeling, though, that sometimes his disappearances come as a surprise to those who sign his paycheque. "I don't know how many times I've been fired at Buffalo," he said with a huge wheezing laugh and a smile so big it actually closes his eyes. "I've been fired one afternoon and Joe will have everyone looking in every bar in town for me the next morning."

JIMMY IS WELL AWARE of the rampie routine. Each van represents a different route in the Buffalo Air Express chain, which Joe began in 1983 to provide the company with a consistent revenue stream. Goods are trucked to Hay River and then flown to Yellowknife, where they continue their distribution. From there, the packages continue their journey. Many are hand-delivered by the rampies to various residences and businesses across Yellowknife. Those bound for the Mackenzie River Valley communities of Déline, Tulita, Norman Wells, and Fort Good Hope are delivered on the Buffalo planes that also carry groceries to those towns throughout the year. Packages destined for communities not on Buffalo's regularly scheduled routes are handed off to Buffalo's partners, which finish the delivery.

The details of this intricate distribution web were lost on me,
though, as I fumbled with package after package, desperately
trying to remember which van serves which part of Yellowknife.

"Kingland Ford?" I cried out as captain A.J. Decoste tossed
me a bumper.

"That's ours!" said Larry as I struggled to find space in
the quickly filling cube van that Larry drives every morning
through the streets of Yellowknife.

"Indian" Jimmy Essery and co-pilot Ian Bottomley guide a pallet loaded
with goods into the belly of an Electra. Ian has made a name for himself at
Buffalo through his commitment, work ethic, and persistence.

The daily grind. c-gwzs is one of the three dc-3s that Buffalo uses for its daily scheduled service between Yellowknife and Hay River. Every morning the plane is unloaded of thousands of pounds of goods—regardless of the temperature.

The scene was one of organized chaos: boxes and packages flying in every direction, the air filled with the smokescreen of localized ice fog, and bleary-eyed rampies calling to one another. The cold, it would seem, affects nobody. Nobody but me, that is. It's hardest on the feet.

"Uh," I mumbled to Larry. "I'm just gonna step inside the hangar for a minute. I, uh, have to interview Mikey."

He eyed me suspiciously, but nodded his assent. Clearly I don't have the rampie work ethic. But I don't want to be a pilot, either, so I'm okay with it.

Rampies who join the Buffalo team are the subject of an informal pool. Other staff members size up the new recruits, then place bets on how long it will take before they quit, the rigours of the job too much for their sorry asses to take. In the rampie odds-making world, I'm a long shot.

My time on the ramp was not intended only to give the boys a helping hand. I was also hoping to impress Joe, show him that I'm not just a pencil-pusher with what the boys up here call "bankers' hands." I'm pretty sure he saw me when he emerged from the cockpit, but just to make sure, I went out of my way to cross paths with him in the hangar. "Morning, Joe!" I exclaimed as cheerfully as possible.

"Morning," he mumbled, giving me as little regard as possible.

"I'm just working out on the ramp if you need me!" I called after him, but it was too late. He disappeared around a corner, and I knew enough not to run after him.

After my too-brief hypothermia-prevention visit to the hangar, I was back on the ramp, finishing the unloading of the "3." Larry and I jumped inside the van (which had warmed up sufficiently to keep my feet from turning blue) and made our first stop at the Buffalo Air Express office, located just around the block from Buffalo's hangar at the Yellowknife airport. After picking up a few more packages, we were off in earnest. Between stops, Larry offered me a rare glimpse into the life and culture of a Buffalo rampie.

Like most rampies who have crossed the tarmac outside Joe's hangar, Larry is in his early twenties and just beginning his career as a pilot. Short, dark, trim, and sporting a thick mop of black hair that seems to have a mind of its own, Larry went to a vocational college in Chicoutimi, Quebec, a small town about 160 kilometres (100 miles) north of Quebec City. Larry had been fortunate enough to be accepted to Cégep de Chicoutimi, one of a number of flight schools in Canada funded by provincial governments. The Canadian flight school experience varies widely. Some people, like Larry, spend two to four years getting a college or university degree that includes

Survival on the Barrens

IF Jimmy can't be found in the Buffalo hangar, chances are he's out on the land pursuing one of his other passions—prospecting, a passion that has landed him in trouble on more than one occasion, like when he was staking claims on the Barrenlands with three other men when a February blizzard blew in. The storm—with temperatures in the low −30°s and a 90-kilometre-an-hour (55-mile-an-hour) wind—got between Jimmy and the others. They were forced to go home, and Jimmy was stuck.

"I spent three days and two nights out on the Barrens, and then I had to walk seventeen miles home. Took me two days, but I did it. I froze both feet, both hands, and my face, but only lost half my left foot."

Amazingly, even though Jimmy had no navigation aids with him, he hit the camp dead-on. "I slept in snowbanks and my clothes got all wet from my breath," he says, not a trace of painful memory on his face as he retells the tale in his raspy voice. "You might think that would be bad, but it saved my life. Because when I came out of the snowbank, my clothes froze and stopped all the wind from going through my clothes."

Back in camp, Jimmy was treated like a man resurrected from the dead. "They came and got me on a [Cessna] 185," he says. "And the pilot looks at me and says 'You're alive! We thought we were gonna have to break your arms just to get your body in the airplane.'"

Jimmy was soon back in Yellowknife, where his first stop was a tub filled with ice water. "They pumped morphine into me and slowly warmed me up," he says. "Then about a week later, they amputated my foot. I waited about a week and then I went back to work."

a pilot's licence. For those who have the financial resources to attend private flight school, the route to the cockpit can be as short as a year.

Either way, Larry knows he's lucky. Most pilots graduate from flight school with debt that can total as much as sixty thousand dollars. Larry wasn't saddled with the same baggage, so instead of looking for a job—*any* job—that would help pay off his debt, Larry went north because he knew it would offer him something a southern Canadian airline couldn't: adventure.

"I wanted to get as far north as I could to get the best experience and become the best pilot that I can be," he told me over the roar of the van's heater fan. "I want to fly with the best." The way Larry sees it, there's no comparison between flying a piece of living history and cruising in a modern aircraft on autopilot.

Larry has the wisdom of someone far older than his twenty years. "Because when you're gonna be forty and sitting in your Airbus 320, you at least want to be thinking that you pushed yourself at some point in your life," he said, talking as if forty is just a step or two away from the grave. I resisted the urge to throttle him. "When your captain asks you what you did before you came to Air Canada, you'd be proud to tell him you flew for Buffalo."

Understandably so. Pilots who survive the Buffalo Airways grist mill and make it to the cockpit are widely respected throughout the aviation world. "If you actually become a captain of one of our planes," Mikey has told me, "you're probably one of the most highly regarded pilots anywhere." Buffalo alumni are now flying for some of the world's most prestigious airlines, in all corners of the globe. "As my dad says, after Buffalo, they never really have to fly again. The plane flies them."

Although the ramp is a fact of life for many flight-school graduates, it's not the only route to the captain's seat, a spot known reverently in the aviation world as the "left seat" (the co-pilot sits in the right seat). After spending a small fortune to get through flight school, some graduates will then shell out an extra eight to ten thousand dollars to get their instructor's licence. Once they are certified instructors, pilots can begin to accrue the holy grail of a pilot's life: hours.

The more hours a pilot has flown, the more proficient he or she is deemed to be. The major North American airlines won't even look at pilots until they have at least a thousand hours under their belt. Novice pilots can accrue precious hours by becoming instructors and taking other would-be flyboys through the air.

Before being handed control of a huge jet, however, most Canadian pilots pay their dues at one of hundreds of small charter airlines dotted across North America. Here they ply their craft on in-between planes like the Beechcraft King Air, Piper PA-31 Navajo, or the de Havilland Canada DHC-6 Twin Otter. Some might jump from there onto a major airline's regional service, where planes such as the Dash 8 are ubiquitous.

For the rest, though, the ramp is the first step to the cockpit. And at Buffalo, the ramp means insanely long work hours in brutal weather conditions. Larry and his compatriots work seven days a week. Their only break comes during the lull between late Saturday morning and Sunday afternoon, because the Hay River–Yellowknife sked doesn't fly Saturday afternoons or Sunday mornings. As we talked about his work schedule, Larry waxed melancholic about the rampies at neighbouring Air Tindi—another Yellowknife company that provides scheduled and charter air services throughout the north—who get four days off for every four days they work.

When I asked Larry to ballpark how many hours he works each week, his eyes glazed over. "I've never figured it out," he said, which I assume is an act of self-preservation. "If I did, I'd probably get Buffalo in trouble." It doesn't take a rocket scientist to do the math, though. By my estimates, these boys are putting in anywhere from sixty to seventy-five hours a week. The million-dollar question, of course, is "Why?"

The answer is surprisingly simple: Larry figures he has to put in his ramp time somewhere, so why not do it at a place where you get to experience flying a piece of living history? "The fact that I'm young makes it easy," he said, thankfully refraining from yet another being-forty-is-just-like-being-dead comment. "I have some responsibilities, but not many. And I don't really mind the hours, because I don't really have a choice. There's no other operator of DC-3s like Buffalo. I had other opportunities. I had a job in Manitoba and one in Quebec and said no to all of them. Because I want to be here."

I want to be here. If there's one anthem that rings consistently from every rampie I meet at Buffalo, it's that. *I want to be here.* And if you don't want to be here, well, you figure it out pretty damn quickly. As Mikey says, the rampies are part of a self-policing wolf pack that answers to its own code of ethics and makes its own rules.

"We rarely have to fire or lay off rampies," Mikey told me one day. "The other guys get rid of them. Because if one guy is slacking, it means the other ones have to work harder. And if they have to work harder, it means they're probably gonna fall behind and get in shit. Because ultimately, we don't give a shit how the job gets done... just get it done." When everyone pulls his own weight, the system works. Make life difficult for the other rampies and it's just a matter of time before you're out the door.

Mikey has spent enough time with rampies and is savvy enough to know how important they are to Buffalo's success. "The heart and soul of Buffalo?" he said. "It isn't me, it isn't Joe, it isn't Rod, and it isn't the pilots. It's the rampies. They're underpaid, they're overworked, and without them, the whole thing collapses.

"I get to hang out in the hangar, answer emails, talk to people," he continued. "But the real guys are out there right now, in minus thirty-five degrees, hauling boxes around town, actually making money for the company." The way Mikey sees it, rampie life is an internship that weeds out the weak from the strong.

The result is what Mikey calls the best pilots in the world. For Joe, it makes perfect sense to demand so much from the rampies. "When you're twenty-five years old, you don't get exhausted," Joe said in a rare moment where he actually made time to talk to me. "You're fireproof and bulletproof and waterproof and inexhaustible."

Good thing, since the rampie internship at Buffalo is anything but easy. Rampies start their careers at Buffalo's operation in Hay River, doing the same work they would in Yellowknife: preparing planes before and after they fly, loading and unloading cargo, and making deliveries and pick-ups around town. Yet in the Buffalo world, Hay River is the minor leagues. If you're ever going to get behind the controls of an airplane, you have to make the jump to the bigs: Yellowknife.

Some rampies will wallow away in Hay River indefinitely, thanks to a personality clash with Joe, poor attitude, less-than-ferocious work ethic, bad luck, or some combination thereof.

Though he has since been laid off, I can't help but think of the case of a rampie from northern British Columbia who for me is the poster boy for how *not* to get ahead at Buffalo.

Like most Buffalo pilot wannabes, Jordan (not his real name) started in Hay River as a junior rampie. Huge and ponderous, Jordan seemed to have the perfect physical attributes for the heavy lifting his new job demanded. But something about him never seemed quite right. He grumbled about his job—a lot. And as Mikey is quick to point out, a quiet rampie is a happy rampie is a rewarded rampie. At Buffalo, the squeaky wheel does not get the grease. Jordan was a squeaky wheel.

Still, Jordan did have opportunities to advance. When the rampie ahead of him was promoted to Yellowknife, he moved to the top of the Hay River food chain; Yellowknife seemed a short step away. Yet the only way he was going to get out of Hay River was to find a suitable replacement to assume his responsibilities. He found one, but when that fell through his attitude worsened. He became dour and mopey. Eventually, Jordan did get to move to Yellowknife to take a flight attending course.

For a rampie, the step from the tarmac to the inside of an airplane is a huge one, regardless of the work. And for Buffalo's rampies, flight attending is the most meaningful way to initiate that process. This is a career move you'd never have to make while working for a southern Canadian airline, but little about Buffalo Airways reflects most airlines' reality. In other words, if you want to get behind the controls of a World War ii legend, you first have to get acquainted with the coffee and the cookies.

Serving drinks and snacks to passengers on the Hay River–Yellowknife run may be a far cry from the romantic notions that most young pilots hold about their profession, but flight attending also gives rampies the chance to see how planes operate. If nothing more, flight attending is a great opportunity to learn the standard operating procedures (sops) of each aircraft.

Jordan took the course, and he even got to sit in the right seat of the dc-3 beside Joe a few times. But his bad karma seemed to follow him across Great Slave Lake. With each opportunity to advance that came Jordan's way, there was something else that held him back. Perhaps not surprisingly, Jordan became one of the hundreds of rampies who never make it though their first year with the company.

High turnover rate is a fact of life at Buffalo, though people usually don't have to be laid off. They just up and quit. Part of the problem is that once pilots graduate from flight school, they realize how few flying jobs there are in Canada. As a result, they send letters of inquiry to virtually every airline imaginable. If Buffalo happens to be the first one to respond positively, they throw themselves into a culture, climate, and geography unlike anything most of them have ever seen. In other words, to last at Buffalo, you have to want to be at Buffalo.

It's a mantra that rings true for everyone who calls the North home, whether temporarily or permanently. The days can get pretty long and lonely in the dead of winter when your heart is somewhere else.

BACK IN THE VAN, Laurent Dussault may be overworked and underpaid, but he complained little as we worked our way through the morning delivering packages. He has a great rapport with his clients and seems willing to do anything to get in the pilot's seat. He knows the opportunity will come.

"You do your ramp time, and at one point they're gonna need a first officer [co-pilot], either because someone leaves or moves up the ladder," he said, handing me a series of boxes for our latest delivery. "At that point they prefer to hire someone they know, someone who's been working on the ramp and has proven themselves, someone they can trust. And that's when they hire a ramp guy. Usually, it's the guy who's worked the hardest or lasted the longest." In most cases, this happens after about a year and a half on the ramp, and culminates with the bronze ring of rampie life: being "checked out."

Being checked out is the pilot's final step to the cockpit, and means he or she has demonstrated enough proficiency with a certain aircraft to be able to fly it. But it's not easy by any stretch of the imagination; the stakes are high and the pressure intense. The process involves a gruelling written exam covering all of the plane's operating systems, followed by a flight test in which multiple stressful scenarios are simulated. Fail either one and it's back to the ramp.

Two young pilots had just been checked out on the DC-3 and were still wearing smiles of success when I arrived at Buffalo. When not busting their humps on the ramp, Graeme Ferguson and Andrew Weich had trained for countless hours on the flight simulator Joe keeps in an upstairs office, where he once ran a flight school called the Buffalo School of Aviation. For Graeme and Andrew, it was a gruelling process: work all day until you're teetering on the edge of exhaustion, fly the "3" on the simulator after hours, then go home and stuff some food down your throat before settling in with the plane's hefty technical manual.

When the big day came, both young pilots had the pleasure of sitting down to a 111-item written exam. As part of this, they had to be ready to answer such questions as:

· What is the purpose of the Wing Flap Relief Valve?
· What is the maximum speed for lowering the landing gear?
· What is the normal operating pressure range of the hydraulic system?
· What is the power source for the surface de-icers?
· What are the operating limits?

Stressful though it may be, the written exam pales in comparison to the air test, when the young pilot sits behind the controls and has to take the plane safely through a series of unfortunate events. Graeme had legendary bush pilot Arnie Schreder, who at the time was Buffalo's chief pilot, in the right seat, with pilot Justin Simle, acting as the examiner, sitting directly behind. Hands shaking, Graeme took the "3" through its paces as the pair threw adversity his way: Engine 2 is failing and has to be shut down—*now* fly the plane. Land the "3" safely in Hay River—*without* using the flaps. Guide the plane through a series of steep bank turns—*and* don't gain or lose more than a hundred feet of altitude in the process.

The mere thought of these scenarios is enough to leave me quaking in my boots, but both Graeme and Andrew passed with flying colours.

And while being checked out is a milestone event for a Buffalo rookie pilot, it doesn't mean life becomes turbulence-free. They still have to sit in the right seat beside Joe on the DC-3. And if Joe McBryan happens to be in a bad mood, God help you.

Larry has worked as a flight attendant during several of Joe's tirades against a rookie pilot. "I was wearing a headset and I could listen to what was happening in the cockpit. And I've heard Joe *unleash* on the first officer."

The bad news is it usually takes at least three years to graduate from co-pilot to a full-fledged captain. And that's only if you're *really* skilled. The good news? You'll learn more from Joe than any other DC-3 captain alive. Better news? You don't have to spend all of your flight time beside Joe, because captains Justin Simle, A.J. Decoste, and Devan Brooks will also be sharing the cockpit with you. And their demeanours are decidedly less surly than that of their mentor, Joe.

As stressful as it may be to have a living aviation legend tear a strip off your quaking hide, Larry figures it's all part of becoming a better pilot. "You've got this guy screaming at you, and you have to stay dead calm and concentrate on flying." That's a task made even more difficult by the retro planes in the Buffalo fleet. They are not easy to fly, and there's certainly no autopilot button.

For Larry, a quiet Joe is a happy Joe. "From my experience, if Joe doesn't talk to you, that's generally a good sign. But if Joe starts yelling, he'll yell at anybody in his path and not about the thing than pissed him off in the first place. He yells about everything that's happening. Let's say you're rolling up an engine tent, he'll unleash on you because the tent is dirty or you're not carrying the seats right."

As difficult as that may prove for a young man, Larry understands that his boss comes by his hard-to-please nature honestly. "That's how old bush pilots are. That's how Joe was taught, and that's how Joe is gonna teach people."

Most Buffalo pilots follow the same flight path as they move up the ranks at Buffalo. After getting checked out on the DC-3, they begin to accumulate precious flying hours sitting beside Joe on the daily sked between Yellowknife and Hay River. From there they move to other missions on the "3," usually cargo runs, this time sitting beside Justin, A.J., or Devan. Then they'll begin to learn the ropes by co-piloting another one of the planes in the Buffalo fleet, whether it be the DC-4, C-46, Electra, or CL-215.

Once they've become sufficiently familiar with a second aircraft they return to the DC-3 in earnest, where they push to accumulate enough hours to become captain. From there they return to their second aircraft to do the same. "Once you're a captain on the '3,' " Mikey says, "it's like you're fast-tracked to be a captain on everything else."

Assuming you can survive Joe, that is. For many rampies, Joe's abrasive exterior can be difficult to handle. Larry takes it in stride. So does David Alexandre, another rampie I spent time with during my induction into the Buffalo family. A Toronto boy through and through, David looked like a rampie long shot when he arrived at Buffalo one cold February afternoon. What people didn't bargain for was his old-world work ethic. Joe's management style? No problem for David.

"The reason I get along with Joe is that he runs the company the same way I was raised as a child," he told me. "My dad is kinda like Joe: very old school. That's why I think I fit in so perfectly here. And if you know you did something wrong, admit to it right away. He'll be mad, but he won't be as mad as if you try to hide it."

Not everyone adjusts to Joe quite as easily as Larry and David have done. "I think there's lot of guys who are used to the new way of life," David said. "You know, technology, your parents can't hit you, this and that. And once those guys come up here, they find that it's very old school. All the stuff that is done by technology in other places is done by manpower at Buffalo. And if you're not used to givin' 'er all the time, it's tough."

AS WE PULLED the van in to the loading dock behind the Yellowknife Walmart for one of our last stops of the morning, Larry informed me that this is where he also eats lunch most days. Given my status as an elder, I chose to eschew the Big Mac combo he opted for, one of the few things he can afford on his rampie salary.

That didn't stop me from enjoying the warmth of the place. As blood flow gradually returned to our toes and fingers, I asked Larry if he planned on making a career out of Buffalo. "No," he said decisively. "For me—and I think for pretty much everyone else—Buffalo is a stepping stone. And I think everyone knows it."

At times he seemed like he had his whole life mapped out. "I came up here to fly these airplanes and spend about five years in total. Then I'll move on to something else. I don't want to make my life in the North. But in the short term, flying these planes is my dream."

6

FLYBOYS

Funny how life works. On the one hand you have a guy like French Larry, twenty years old and with his life seemingly mapped out. For Larry, Buffalo may be a stepping stone to something else, but his short-term dream is to fly the vintage propliners that make Buffalo unique.

Then there's Justin Simle, chief pilot at Buffalo and favourite of many women who watch *Ice Pilots*. The way Justin tells it, his arrival at Buffalo was not quite as well planned as Larry's. Yet here he is, ten years later, having forged a career for himself as one of the world's most accomplished young pilots of World War II aircraft.

If there is one person other than Mikey who has seen his personal stock rise as a result of the *Ice Pilots* phenomenon, it's Justin. Standing about six feet tall and thin as a rake, Justin oozes frontier cool. His square jaw is punctuated by a deep cleft in his chin, and his big brown eyes look right through you. No matter where we went, Justin was recognized—and apparently loved. From shop clerks to the waitresses in the diners where we ate our lunches, the ladies all seemed to have a kind word for Justin, and he for them.

I first met Justin in the Pilots' Lounge at the Buffalo hangar. Like everything else about Joe McBryan and the world he's created, the Lounge harkens back to an earlier age. Its style is distinctly retro. Yet it doesn't take a Debbie Travis or Martha Stewart to realize that while the Lounge is not long on tasteful furnishings, it is functional and serves a real-world purpose. Like Joe himself, there is no pretense about the place. It is what it is and does what it does. If you don't like it, get the hell out.

Three desks and chairs line the perimeter of the room; they sit under a series of old shelves sagging under the weight of dozens of technical publications: crew resource management (CRM) manuals, GPS manuals, approved check pilot courses, training manuals, and study guides for the various planes in the Buffalo fleet: the DC-3, the DC-4, the C-46, the Electra, and the CL-215. A window looks out onto the hangar.

When they're not flying or running around doing the hundreds of other chores that comprise their day-to-day lives, the Lounge is where you'll find Buffalo's pilots. Here they pass the time between flights, entering data into log books or brushing up on the technical aspects of the planes they command. If Justin is in the hangar, chances are he's in the Lounge.

From what I can tell, Justin is about as far away from Joe as a human can possibly be—on the outside. He is warm and engaging, and rarely—if ever—loses his cool. Not that he hasn't

One of the best-loved episodes of *Ice Pilots* saw the crew transport the Stanley Cup across the North, documenting Mikey McBryan's love affair with the trophy in the bargain. Here chief pilot Justin Simle poses with the iconic cup.

had the opportunity to. Justin has been flying with Buffalo since May 29, 2001, his twenty-first birthday. He has had his share of close calls and exciting experiences. Buffalo may be "only" a small airline operating out of a small town in northern Canada, but it has afforded a guy like Justin the opportunity to see and do things he may otherwise have only dreamed about, such as his inclusion on a team charged with transporting two short-range CL-215 water bombers on a 12,000-kilometre (7,500-mile) odyssey from Yellowknife to Ankara, Turkey.

Production of the Canadair CL-215 water bomber (affectionately known as "the Duck" to those who fly her) began in 1969, the first in a series of firefighting flying boats built by Bombardier, the Canadian civil and military aircraft manufacturer. Though production of the Duck stopped in 1989, the planes are still widely used today throughout northern Canada as well as a number of other countries, including Italy, Thailand, Turkey, Serbia, France, Greece, and the United States. Bombardier currently builds the CL-415, a bigger, more powerful turboprop version of the CL-215.

Contrary to what most people think, the primary responsibility of the 215 in firefighting operations is *not* to put out fires, but to reduce their intensity, thereby giving ground crews a chance to attack the fire using hand pumps, chainsaws, axes, and other hand tools. The 215 can scoop some 5,000 litres (1,320 gallons) of water off nearby water sources (rivers, lakes, oceans) at airspeeds between 140 and 150 kilometres an hour (87–93 miles per hour). The 215 needs a water source about 1.5 kilometres (1 mile) long and 2 metres (2 yards) deep; it can fill its tanks in about ten seconds and empty them in one. Typically, the planes are also equipped with foam-injection equipment that mixes the water with fire-retardant foam. Assuming a suitable water source is close by, the Duck can deliver as many as 125 loads of water and retardant in a single day.

The 215 is a marvel of engineering technology. The craft is designed to take off and land on short, remote airstrips, and operates efficiently at low speeds. Its high wings offer its crew greater visibility over water sources and drop zones, which can mean the difference between success and disaster in the insanely difficult conditions its pilots often fly. The plane is easy to manoeuvre in the heavy gusts, violent updrafts, and fierce turbulence that characterize forest fires. No wonder the Turks wanted the two planes so badly; production of the 215s stopped in 1990, and the planes are not easy to come by, a result of their utility and palatable price tag.

CL-215 Facts & Figures

- CAPACITY: Two flight crew and 18 passengers (utility version)
- PRODUCTION: 125
- PAYLOAD: 5,346 litres (1,176 imperial gallons) of water or 6,123 kilograms (12,000 pounds) of chemicals
- LENGTH: 19.82 metres (65 feet)
- WINGSPAN: 28.6 metres (93 feet, 10 inches)
- HEIGHT: 8.98 metres (29 feet, 6 inches)
- MAXIMUM SPEED: 605 km/h (376 MPH)
- CRUISE SPEED: 291 km/h (181 MPH)
- RANGE: 2,260 kilometres (1,405 miles)
- EMPTY WEIGHT: 12,065 kilograms (26,600 pounds)
- MAXIMUM TAKEOFF WEIGHT: 17,100 kilograms (37,700 pounds) from water and 19,730 kilograms (43,500 pounds) from land

FOR BUFFALO JOE, the water bomber deal could not have come at a better time, as Buffalo was struggling financially after worldwide recession struck in 2008. The Turkish government contacted Buffalo, interested in buying the two planes, a deal that could add as much as seven million dollars in revenue to the Buffalo coffers. It's not the kind of business transaction Buffalo usually engages in, but these were tough times and Joe needed the money to keep the company on solid financial footing.

Once the deal was sealed, the Buffalo crew had one major hurdle to leap: the Atlantic Ocean. The CL-215 is a short-range, low-flying aircraft designed to scoop water out of lakes and dump it on nearby fires. Crossing vast expanses of open ocean? Not part of the plan. CL-215s are essentially flying boats, but they are not designed to withstand the high waves of the open sea, nor do they have the fuel capacity to cross it. Yet with seven million dollars on the line, Joe and his team were willing to get creative.

Joe turned the task of crossing the Atlantic to long-time mechanic Cory Dodd, a Winnipeg native who has been with Buffalo since 1993. Cory had to find a way to modify the CL-215s to get them across 2,000 kilometres (1,200 miles) of open ocean between St. John's, Newfoundland, and Portugal's Azores Islands, a ten-hour flight. The solution came in the form

The CL-215 is perfectly designed for scooping water off lakes and dumping it over nearby fires. The planes are highly sought after by countries with vast stretches of forest, a fact Buffalo Joe was undoubtedly aware of when he sold two of them to the Turkish government.

of two 1,890-litre (500-gallon) rubber bladders installed in the cabin of each CL-215 and connected to the plane's main fuel system.

With the question of *how* to get the planes to Turkey seemingly solved, Joe next had to decide *who* would take the trip. It was little surprise he chose Justin, who at that point had eight years of Buffalo service under his belt. Justin was lucky enough to be sharing the controls of his plane with Arnie Schreder, a bush pilot legend, Justin's mentor, and then the chief pilot of Buffalo Airways. Two guns for hire—Dave "Rooster" Poole and George Furey—flew the second plane.

FOR ARNIE, anticipating what might happen *after* the expedition to Turkey was just too much to ask given the risks inherent in the venture. The trip began with a six-hour flight to Winnipeg, a normally casual jaunt made stressful by the fact that the 215s do not have aircraft radar on board and need to be flown under what is known as Visual Flight Rules, or VFR. VFR is a set of regulations that permits pilots to operate aircraft only in weather that is clear enough for them to see where they're going. If clouds set in or the ceiling drops, they're out of luck. To make matters worse, the 215s have no de-icing equipment, since they are exclusively flown in the summer, and their fat wings are an easy target for ice formation, which has caused the untimely demise of more than one pilot.

The next leg of the journey saw the 215s travel from Winnipeg to Montreal, Quebec—a 14-hour, 1,800-kilometre (1,100 mile) flight—followed by 1,600 kilometres (1,000 miles) to St. John's, Newfoundland, the easternmost city in North America. Arnie thought the trip over mainland Canada would represent the most difficult part of the journey to Turkey, and in some respects he was right. But he could not have anticipated what he and the rest of the crew would encounter while in St. John's, an event that would forever change their perspective on open-ocean flying.

With the formidable journey staring them in the face, the crew knew they had to be as prepared as possible for anything the North Atlantic might throw at them.

"You'd be an idiot to not know what can happen before you take that trip," Justin told me. "And if you didn't know what could happen and you agreed to do that trip, you're stupid."

The North Atlantic is characterized by thousands of kilometres of featureless expanses of water, as well as unpredictable, violent weather. It has claimed its share of air disaster victims, beginning in May 1927 with the deaths of aviators Charles Nungesser and François Coli, who crashed while trying to cross the ocean from Paris to the United States in a Levasseur PL. 8 biplane. On February 2, 1953, a Skyways Avro York disappeared over the North Atlantic; neither the plane nor its thirty-nine passengers were ever seen again.

Those incidents were likely swirling in the back of the minds of Justin and his colleagues as they began their transatlantic preparations in St. John's. Among other things, the crew spent some time participating in a survival-training course, just in case they had to "ditch," or make an emergency landing on water. When a plane ditches—whether because of engine failure or weather conditions—the pilot's main concern is bringing the plane to a level landing on the water without destroying the aircraft. Ditchings are rare among commercial craft, but they occur fairly often in other kinds of aviation. Perhaps the most famous successful ditching in recent history occurred on January 15, 2009, when US Airways Flight 1549 struck a flock of Canada geese after takeoff from LaGuardia Airport and then safely landed in the Hudson River. All 155 passengers and crew survived.

Staving off hypothermia is a major concern in open-ocean ditchings, and the only way to preserve body heat is by wearing a high-tech survival suit, which Justin, Arnie, George, and Dave did for the first time in St. John's. The bright orange suits are heavy, tight, and rubbery and cover the entire body from the ankles to the neck—almost claustrophobic. They not only make it difficult to move freely, they're hotter than hell. The crew realized that they'd have no chance in the icy waters of the North Atlantic without the suits: the orange cocoons would have to stay on for the entire ocean crossing to Santa Maria, one of the Azores Islands.

With the crew trained in the fine details of North Atlantic survival, the waiting game began. For the 215s to complete the flight successfully, three things needed to occur simultaneously: clear skies, a tail wind, and temperatures above freezing.

Just as Justin and his colleagues were feeling good about their chances of making it unscathed to Santa Maria, disaster struck: a Sikorsky S-92 helicopter carrying eighteen workers to an off-shore oil platform ditched fifty kilometres (thirty miles) east of St. John's. Only one survivor was found.

The tragedy highlighted the sometimes precarious nature of flying over open ocean, yet Justin and the others remained focused on the job. When all three conditions were finally met, the planes took off on what may have been the most dangerous flight of Justin's and Arnie's careers. "When you look below you and see fifty-foot swells rolling... that's something to see," Justin said.

Too Close for Comfort

AFTER Buffalo delivered two CL-215 water bombers to Turkish government officials in Ankara, Arnie Schreder stayed on for a while to teach the eager Turkish pilots how to fly them. Each young pilot would take the plane up for a spin, then bring it down for a landing.

Ice Pilots videographer Todd Craddock stationed himself at the far end of the runway, filming the takeoffs and landings. All was going well until one pilot forgot to lower the landing gear as he approached the runway. The bottom of the 215's fuselage scraped horribly against the runway, showering it with sparks and filling the air with the ungodly shriek of metal. Craddock stood at the end of the runway filming the incident, until he thought the plane was going to plow into him, forcing him to run for his life. Fortunately, the pilot was able to compose himself, pull up from the runway, and get the 215 airborne again.

As stressful as the flight was for Justin, the 215s made it to the tiny airstrip on Santa Maria without incident. That night, the crew celebrated its success with a night on the town in Vila do Porto, population 5,500. "It was sure nice to put that big chunk of ocean behind you," he adds.

With the most dangerous leg of the journey over, the crew looked forward to the second over-ocean portion of their trip, the 1,300 kilometres (800 miles) between Santa Maria and Cascais on mainland Portugal, a six-hour flight. Given their ease of passage between St. John's and Santa Maria, everyone decided to leave the survival suits in the back of the plane for the second leg.

Perhaps the decision was made a bit too hastily. Only an hour out of Santa Maria, the 215 piloted by George and Dave experienced a dangerous phenomenon known as an "engine overspeed" on its left engine. When an overspeed occurs, the engine and propeller turn far faster than they are designed to do, either by pilot error or by mechanical malfunction. The pilots lost complete control of the left engine, forcing them to turn back to Santa Maria and make an emergency landing.

As Justin tells it, the overspeed was no laughing matter: "An engine failure in a CL-215 at that weight and those cold temperatures is a serious deal." Indeed. With only one engine working, a 215 cannot stay airborne for long, and the stress on the hobbled engine is incredible. Imagine driving your car as fast as it can go and then slamming it into first gear. The worst-case scenario with an engine overspeed? The propeller sheds its blades, which then rip through the plane's fuselage.

In the meantime, Justin and Arnie were safe in Cascais, waiting for their counterparts to arrive. When it became obvious that the second water bomber would be delayed in Santa Maria awaiting replacement parts, Arnie and Justin made their way to Ankara, Turkey, via Spain and Malta. It was only half the agreed-upon delivery, but their clients were thrilled to have even one 215 on home soil. The second plane arrived a few days later, to the delight of the Turks.

THOUGH THE CL-215 ODYSSEY would rank as one of the most unusual missions Arnie Schreder flew in thirty years of contract flying with Buffalo, comprising almost forty thousand hours, nothing could have prepared Arnie for his last revenue flight (a flight the pilot gets paid for, as opposed to a training or mechanical checkup flight) with Buffalo. Enter *Dambusters*.

To many people, the term "dambusters" has a historical context, thanks to one of the most daring and immortalized raids carried out during World War II. On May 16, 1943, nineteen British Lancaster bombers took off from a little-known airfield in Lincolnshire, en route to three heavily defended reservoirs in Germany. Their mission: destroy three dams deep in Germany's industrial heartland, thereby crippling the German army. To do so they used a 4,175-kilogram (9,200-pound) bomb designed specifically to bounce off the water and explode once it impacted the dam. Two dams were destroyed, the third badly damaged.

Since that day, the feat has been attempted only once, as a U.S. military experiment in 1946 that went horribly wrong when the bomb bounced too high off the water and destroyed the plane that had just dropped it. Until Arnie, that is.

After six months of work by one of the world's foremost authorities on spinning objects—not to mention the fifty-odd other people who helped bring it all together—a British production team called on Arnie to drop the newly designed bomb (designed *not* to explode) from a Buffalo DC-4 to see if the raid could be replicated for a made-for-TV special called *Dambusters*. The stakes were unbelievably high: despite lots of practice runs, Arnie would only have one shot at the real thing. One mistake—which could see the bomb bounce high off the water and tear the DC-4 to shreds—could mean his death.

"Nothing went right," Mikey said. "In fact, the *only* thing that went right was the last moment, when Arnie dropped the bomb and it skipped over the water—right into the dam! Those were probably the best four seconds of my life. There's not very many things in life you work that hard on for four seconds of reward."

Arnie wasn't the only one putting himself at risk that day. According to Mikey, it's the most dangerous thing he's ever done too. "We had people all over the place, and that bomb could have gone anywhere. But Arnie just comes in and tick, tick—bang! Dead centre. If he had a hundred more tries, I don't know if he could do it as perfectly."

It was the last revenue flight the legendary Arnie has ever flown for Buffalo.

"What a way to go out," said Mikey.

EXPERIENCES SUCH AS THESE may be par for the course for a Buffalo flyboy who reaches the exalted status of chief pilot, but they are anything but normal for the greenhorn, as Justin was when he first arrived on the Buffalo scene back in 2001. And yet, something about Justin seems, well, special. It's almost as if he's meant to be where he is.

You might have even guessed that back on Justin's twenty-first birthday. There he was, his first day at Buffalo, and on the sked down to Hay River that evening, Joe let him take control of the DC-3. "That was my birthday present," he told me.

Yet just like the young men he works with today, Justin had to put in his time on the ramp before he could graduate to the upper echelon of the Buffalo hierarchy. He was checked out on the DC-3 on April 7, 2002. I'm not sure if it speaks to deep-rooted psychological scarring from spending so much time with Joe, but Justin can remember, almost to the minute, how much time he spent beside Joe on the DC-3. "I flew with Joe for thirteen months, one week, and three days," he tells me. "And then they checked me out on the DC-4 on my twenty-third birthday, May 29, 2003."

In classic Buffalo fashion, Justin did whatever was necessary to keep the company running, even after he'd reached the exalted status of pilot. He told me about his early days in Yellowknife, when Buffalo was having difficulty finding long-haul truck drivers to courier goods between Hay River and Edmonton.

"I'd fly the sked across the lake in the morning, from Hay to Yellowknife, then sleep the afternoon in Yellowknife, from noon until around 3 PM," he said. "When I woke up, I'd get the sked ready, fly back to Hay River and unload it. Then I'd get in the long-haul truck, drive halfway down to Edmonton, and meet the guy driving north from Edmonton in Dixonville, Alberta. We'd run across the road and switch trucks:

" 'How's it running?'

" 'Good!'

" 'How's it running?'

" 'Good!' "

Justin would hop in the truck and finish the twelve-hour drive back to Hay River, where he would load his truckful of goods back on to the sked, fly it to Yellowknife, and get a few hours of sleep before starting the entire process over again.

This type of ridiculous work ethic is a simple fact of life at Buffalo. At first blush, it may seem harsh, even draconian. But to the people who make their living here, there are benefits as well. "All the people who work here are really close," Justin says. "You're working pretty hard and you spend a lot of time with the people you work with. So they become like your friends; you hang out with them after work too."

If anything, the conditions at Buffalo mean your co-workers are generally good people. As Justin explains it, prima donnas don't last very long in Yellowknife. "It's a tough place to make a living; it's not for everybody. The benefit is that you don't get assholes here. Because everyone has gotta work hard and work together, eh?"

The deeply furrowed landscape of Ellesmere Island seems like the last place anybody would want to land a plane. Yet Buffalo's business has taken its pilots here many times, usually to military research stations at Eureka and Alert in Nunavut.

Though the benefits of such an arrangement are obvious, it comes at a price too: as Scott Blue described to me one evening in a Yellowknife restaurant, having a social life outside of Buffalo is nearly impossible. "The thing that really gets to me at Buffalo is that I've become sick and tired of turning down weekends in Calgary or back home in Toronto, or not being able to have time off when I want it." Scott's life is one where being on call is a constant bedfellow, his plans are subject to change at a moment's notice.

Such conditions don't make it easy to have a relationship. "I tried dating girls when I first got here, but I never knew when I would be shipped off somewhere or gone. So they all got bored and found someone else."

As troublesome as they may be, these sacrifices are worth it to Scotty, who—like most of his Buffalo comrades—has seen and done things most pilots will never experience. "It's really a crazy place," he says with a conspiratorial smile. "I remember my first summer flying to Sawmill Bay [on Great Bear Lake, some 400 kilometres or 250 miles northwest of Yellowknife] and landing a DC-3 on a strip that had hardly seen a plane in years. The year before, they had taken a DC-3 in there, and the props were ripping through trees when they landed." Scott spent part of the day exploring the camp—which has seen varied uses over the decades, including timber sawmill, loading dock, and air force airfield—along with the machinery, vehicles, and buildings left behind when it was abandoned in 1987.

Experiences like that may not be routine, but they're commonplace enough to keep a guy like Scott content to call Buffalo home for the foreseeable future. "I could go somewhere else," he says, hinting that some of Canada's major airlines have already made overtures to him. "But where else could I fly a c-46 to Eureka?"

Good point. Even for those of us fortunate enough to have spent time in the North, Eureka is the remotest of the remote. A small research base set on southern Ellesmere Island in the far northern reaches of Nunavut (79°59' N latitude), Eureka is the second-northernmost permanent research station in the world. Only Alert—perched on the northern tip of Ellesmere Island—is farther north.

"Back in the day, it was routine to get piston-pounding airplanes that far north. But now they just don't go up there anymore. So it may be one of the last—if not the last—times a c-46 goes that far north. I'll never forget doing that; it was unbelievable."

So for all the heartache that comes along with being part of the Buffalo family, it also offers its pilots adventures of the most far-flung kind. Today, *Ice Pilots* has helped give young pilots a glimpse into the kinds of adventures awaiting them north of 60. Like Scotty, though, Justin didn't have the luxury of knowing before he arrived what the company was like. So when Justin first showed up at Buffalo's door, he had no idea what was awaiting him on the other side.

AS WITH MOST Buffalo pilots, Justin's route to Yellowknife was anything but straightforward, though he was long fascinated with the idea of flying. Justin was born just outside of Langley, British Columbia, but it wasn't long before his parents started dragging him all over the world as different business opportunities presented themselves.

"We spent some time in Saudi Arabia," he told me over lunch one day at the Gold Range Diner, a Yellowknife institution and one of Justin's favourite lunch-hour dining spots. The Gold Range Diner epitomizes the dichotomy of modern-day Yellowknife. From the outside, it's rundown, maybe even a little grotty. The bright yellow building has seen better days. The paint is peeling, the wooden steps worn. The interior— with its brick-coloured linoleum floor and Asian decor—feels and smells like a building past its prime. Sit down for a while, though, and you see what really makes the place tick. Here are people from all walks of Yellowknife life—blue collar and white collar, Native and non-Native—enjoying surprisingly good food in a friendly and welcoming atmosphere. The first time Justin and I sat down in the diner, I was shocked to enjoy one of the best chicken curries I'd had in a long time.

"We also lived in Oman," he continued. "When I was five we moved to Dubai, and we lived there for two years." The rest of Justin's childhood reads like pages from the Canadian atlas: six months in Rossland, British Columbia; four years in Vancouver; three years in Ottawa; four years in Winnipeg; six months in Castlegar, British Columbia; and eighteen months in Edmonton.

The idea of flying always fascinated Justin, so when he was fifteen—and didn't yet have a driver's licence—his mother began diligently driving him to the airport for lessons. He

The Gold Range

LOCATED in the heart of downtown Yellowknife, the Gold Range Hotel and bar is the most infamous drinking establishment in the Canadian North. From Taloyoak to Tuktoyaktuk, everyone knows about the "Strange Range."

Over the years, the Gold Range has played host to a number of business ventures, including a strip joint, boarding house, and the rough-and-tumble bar that exists to this day. It's not uncommon to walk by the place—day or night—and see a couple of patrons drunkenly fighting on the sidewalks outside. In the mid-1980s, its general manager claimed that the bar sold more beer than any other in Canada.

Yet there's more to the Gold Range than its nefarious reputation suggests. It's a working-man's bar, yes, but a meeting place too. In years gone by, if you wanted to find out which company was hiring labourers or needed to pass information along, the Range was the place to do it.

During my time at Buffalo, the City of Yellowknife announced its intention to buy a chunk of real estate on 50th Street, including the Gold Range, as part of a plan to clean up downtown.

Cleaner? Perhaps. Less interesting? Most definitely.

soon got his private pilot's licence, and then spent two years at Mount Royal College (now Mount Royal University) in Calgary. With a crisp new commercial pilot's licence in his hand and a fresh outlook on life, Justin took the road north to Yellowknife for the same reason that hundreds of other young, eager Buffalo pilots have: there were no jobs anywhere else.

"About thirty-five people graduated from my class in flight school," he explained. "And from that class, maybe ten of us are working now. So if you wanted a job, you had to do what it took."

That's exactly what Justin did. "I threw all my worldly possessions in the back of my Mustang—one suitcase, a sleeping bag, and a box of assorted shit—and started driving north," he told me.

JUSTIN STRUCK ME as the kind of guy who will stop at nothing to makes his dreams happen, having done everything necessary to get himself what he considers the best flying gig on Earth. For Justin, there is no place he'd rather be—at least right now. "I guess I'll have to grow up and get a real job eventually," he said with a wry smile. "But until then, I'll just keep doing this."

A combination of things keeps him at Buffalo. "As a pilot, you develop a real connection with these planes. It's something special, and it's so different."

It's the land too. "The North is so huge, so raw, so beautiful. There's hardly anybody that lives here, and there's so much to see. I've flown planes across the world at low levels. And there are some beautiful places, but there's no place in the world like the North. It's harsh, and it's a dangerous place that can kill you. But it's beautiful."

And even though he is sitting right in front of me in his customary seat in a noisy diner, Justin went away for a few seconds. I could see it in his eyes, hear it in his voice. "In the fall, the tundra turns red for about a week right before the snow flies. You're flying over the ground and there's muskox and caribou everywhere. Even now after doing it for ten years, the beauty of it is never lost on me."

7

THE LAND
BEFORE TIME

Another night at Surly Bob's.

I can't remember how long ago we descended the narrow staircase to this subterranean temple to sports and greasy food, but if time is measured in Coronas, it's been a while. Yet even though my eyesight is becoming fuzzier with each bottle, I can still appreciate the surroundings. From the outside, Surly Bob's doesn't look like a hell of a lot. In fact, the hand-painted sign on an otherwise nondescript stone-faced building is easily overlooked, except for the rather surly looking bird painted on the door.

Like so many things in Yellowknife, though, the cover doesn't do justice to the rest of the book, and Surly Bob's is no different. The sports bar may be just a square room with various flat-screen TVs dotting the walls, but Bob (who, as

it turns out, isn't that surly) serves up traditional pub-style dishes like burgers and sandwiches, fish 'n' chips, fajitas, soups, and salads at reasonable prices. And like so many small-town places of this vintage, it's almost impossible to step into the place without meeting someone you know. Especially when you're with Mikey McBryan, a man whose popularity rises exponentially on Wednesday nights... *Ice Pilots* nights.

Mikey is sitting across from me, the outline of his head becoming fuzzier with each bucket of Coronas that Bob delivers to the table. I've never been a drinker, so I shouldn't be particularly surprised that Mikey is way ahead of me on the beer front. But I never would have expected the prodigious rate at which he packs them away. I'm into my fifth; Mikey has probably doubled my count.

While I'm barely coherent, Mikey seems unaffected by the alcohol now coursing through his veins. Unless you count the number of times he says *fuck*, that is. Here in Yellowknife—particularly in the Buffalo hangar—the word gets a fair bit of airtime. And as the number of beers consumed increases, so does the number of times the word pops up in our speech. I like to call it the Fuck Quotient.

Swear words notwithstanding, Mikey is still as lucid as ever. Actually, he sounds smarter than ever to me as we talk about how Yellowknife is the perfect place for Buffalo to call home.

"We don't pick Yellowknife," he says. "I mean does anyone really wanna be in minus fuckin' fifty degrees every day? Would I rather be in Vegas doing this? Yes. But in Vegas you've got to compete with trucks, which is a far superior form of transportation."

"Wait a second. Are you saying trucks are superior to airplanes?"

"Pound for pound, air travel is one of the most inefficient ways of delivering cargo," he says. "Assuming you've got an airport that can handle it, the most you can haul with an airplane is about forty thousand pounds. A truck can take sixty thousand pounds. And don't even talk about boats. You can put millions of pounds on a boat.

"So leaving the ground actually has a lot of negatives. There's reasons why airplanes don't haul cargo like they used to. A truck can haul three times as much, operate with one driver and can deliver for pennies a pound. Airplanes cost dollars per pound to ship."

In some respects, it's surprising to hear Mikey talk so disparagingly about air cargo. At least half of Buffalo's annual revenue comes from shipping goods from Point A to Point B (the other half being very lucrative summer firefighting contracts with the government). On any given day, there's likely a Buffalo aircraft soaring over northern skies with a planeload of mining equipment, food, building materials, or fuel.

Unlike the flagship airlines that operate in Canada (Air Canada and WestJet come to mind), most of Buffalo's cargo transportation happens on planes used exclusively for that purpose. So while other airlines might dedicate a bit of empty space on a passenger plane for cargo, Buffalo fills entire planes with the stuff.

It may not be as glamorous as hauling people around, but that's quite all right with Mikey. "There's a reason why a shit truck driver earns more than a cabbie: nobody wants to haul shit round. So that's basically what we are: flying shit trucks."

That's an oversimplification, considering the sheer volume of stuff Buffalo hauls. Mikey figures the company moves at least five million pounds of cargo every year. The c-46 probably accounts for three million pounds of cargo annually, at thirteen thousand pounds four times each week for fifty-two weeks.

Yet predicting how much cargo Buffalo will haul in any given year is as unpredictable as Joe's temper. "You could do one job that could be two million pounds," Mikey says. "And if you get a good contract—like a diamond mine when they're starting out—you could do two million *tons*."

Despite that, Mikey believes ships and trucks are ultimately killing the aviation industry. "The only thing keeping planes in the air is overnight freight," he says through a mouthful of chicken wing. "With Internet ordering, everyone wants it here *now*. That's what keeps aviation alive. You order that hoodie or sweatshirt online and you want it in Canmore the next day, it has to go on an airplane."

The X factor in Mikey's equation is one he is well acquainted with: the North. In the North, towns are small and road-building is prohibitively expensive. All of a sudden, air travel becomes more attractive than in more populated areas. "Let's say it costs about a million dollars a mile to build a decent road," Mikey says, stuffing a lime into a Dos Equis and handing it to me. "If a community is five hundred miles away and there's four hundred people in it, that's a million dollars per person to bring in cargo. So in the short term, it's much cheaper to fly stuff in. If the community had 400,000 people living in it, you wouldn't even think about it. You would build the road out of necessity, since it would be physically impossible to fly everything in."

Permanent roads are few and far between in Canada's northern reaches, so Buffalo is there to fill the gaps. That's why the system works so well: there's a niche for Buffalo in the North. It's one of the last places in the world where the company could exist in its present form.

Maybe it's the stunned look on my face, my glassy eyes, or the drool beginning to form around the edges of my mouth, but Mikey feels a need to explain with an analogy. "You know the movie *The Land Before Time,* where they were trying to find Paradise Valley? That's where we are. We're in that last nook where the dinosaurs are surviving. But they won't survive forever, just like we won't. We've only survived because we're sheltered between two canyons."

I'm skeptical. Sure, operating in a secluded place may have helped Buffalo succeed, but it's not the *only* reason the company has managed to thrive through good times and bad. These guys know what their core business is, and they do it well—really well. How else do you explain flying around in planes whose designers, builders, and first pilots are long dead and gone?

Explanation #1: They know where to get parts.

"Over ten thousand DC-3s were built, so there's ten thousand of every part out there somewhere," Mikey says. "And that's just on the airplanes, let alone the parts they built to support those airplanes." Compare that with a plane like the Electra, which saw only 170 built before production stopped in 1961. Talk about an impossible undertaking; try finding parts for *that* plane.

Not surprisingly, Buffalo's Yellowknife hangar has its own machining facility to help when pre-made parts cannot be found. "We can do everything here except the engines, landing gear, and instrumentation," Mike says.

Explanation #2: They know where to find mechanics.

Quick quiz: What's easier for Mikey to find, new pilots or new mechanics? If you answered *new pilots,* you're wrong. "It's ten times more difficult to find mechanics than pilots," Mikey says. "Pilots are literally a dime a dozen. If I wanted a pilot to fly a DC-3, one would show up tomorrow. But if you said you

Born in Winnipeg, thirty-four-year-old mechanic James Dwojak has seen his fair share of breakdowns during his ten years at Buffalo. James knows as well as anybody that to be a successful airplane mechanic in the North, you have to be tough, tenacious, and versatile.

needed someone to work on a DC-3, you're gonna have to go find him somewhere or pull him out of jail. With mechanics, it's not like we need *a* guy, it's like we need *that* guy!"

Clearly, the solution does not come as easily as placing a Help Wanted ad in a newspaper. "We'd get people answering the ad, but they'd have no experience," Mikey says. "You can teach a pilot to fly a DC-3 in ten hours. But in ten hours you know *nothing* about the mechanics of a DC-3." Luckily, Buffalo has built enough of a reputation in a small enough industry that skilled mechanics often find them.

Explanation #3: They have a hell of a lot of experience working on vintage planes.

Don't ask Mikey McBryan if maintaining a vintage plane is any easier than maintaining a twenty-first-century jet. He'll tell you the question is out of context, and context is everything.

"It's easier for Buffalo, because we know what we're doing. If you sent a DC-3 to WestJet and asked them to fix it, it would take up all their time. Put a 737 in here and it would take all our time. It's not like new airplanes don't have problems, but you can go to the Walmart of schools and learn how to fix it. Plug it into a computer and the computer fixes it. But with a DC-3, DC-4, or C-46, you're working on something that you can't go to school for. You've gotta work on it to learn."

Explanation #4: They know where to get the planes.

"Airplanes are easy," Mikey says. "Just go to an airport and you'll find an airplane."

Although not quite as simple as that, the airline industry is a tightly knit one, which allows for a fair bit of shared information. As Mikey tells me, more often than not, the planes find Buffalo, not vice versa. That doesn't mean he hasn't had to invoke his own ingenuity to track down Buffalo's latest purchase. In one well-known *Ice Pilots* episode, Mikey finds a CL-215 water bomber using Google Earth and travels to remote Venezuela to finish the deal. More recently, he bought one in North Carolina—through eBay.

IT WAS AROUND MIDNIGHT when I stumbled out of Surly Bob's and made my way back to Mikey's place, hoping not to become one of those grim northern legends: a drunk who falls asleep in a snowbank in the middle of a Yellowknife winter night, never to wake up again. For his part, Mikey hooked up with a few friends at Surly's and made his way to Harley's, excited that it was Monday, the day they introduce the new stripper for the week. He didn't get home until around three in the morning, but when Tuesday rolled around, it was me who slept in and then nursed the dull ache of a hangover, while Mikey was at the hangar at 7:30 A M as always, making ready to meet his dad when the sked rolled down the runway.

Alone at the house, I had the opportunity to explore Mikey's crib. Actually, from what I can gather, it's not Mikey's crib at all. Not exclusively, that is.

"You can crash at my place if you want," Justin said to me one day.

"Thanks, but I'm good. I'm staying at Mikey's place."

"You mean *Joe's* place."

Whatever. I'd venture to guess that Joe actually owns the place, but it's where Mikey hangs his hat during those rare moments he's not at the hangar, so for me it's Mikey's Place. Joe stays there too, but only on weekends between the Saturday morning sked from Hay River and the one returning there late Sunday afternoon. That's when I get the hell out.

Either way, the place is a stereotypical bachelor pad. It sits on McAvoy Road, a narrow, winding gravel pathway that hugs outcrops of grey rock as it makes its way along Back Bay, a protected arm of Great Slave Lake. Ironically enough, McAvoy Road is named for a well-known Yellowknife family of bush pilots and diamond drillers, the very family that gave the world Chuck McAvoy, one of the most influential personalities in young Joe McBryan's life. Mikey's house—a place he likes to call the "Den of Solitude," given his penchant for avoiding visitors (even trick-or-treaters)—sits directly beside his brother Rod's and forms the foundation of Buffalo's Yellowknife float-plane base.

Surrounding the two houses—Rod and his wife Sasha's tidy grey mobile home and Mikey's rambling two-storey house—is nothing but gravel. It's not the most natural environment, but it's low maintenance. You won't find any garden gnomes here. In fact, with the amount of machinery and equipment scattered around the place, it feels like we haven't really left the hangar at all.

Luckily, that ambience stops at Mikey's door, where the decor changes from workyard to bachelor reno chic. The front door opens to a den of sorts, though Mikey uses it mostly for storage. A pair of couches lie partially buried under assorted books, clothes, boxes, and rarely used exercise equipment. A hallway at the far end of the room leads to a series of small bedrooms. Upstairs is the main living area, where an open

Old and older. The Electra in the foreground seems positively modern compared to the DC-4 in the background. The DC-4 is the only plane in the Buffalo fleet powered by four engines.

kitchen, dining room, and living room all seem to face Mikey's flat-screen TV. All around are signs of work in progress: a wall cut open here, a bathroom being rebuilt there. Mikey's bedroom is on the top floor.

The fridge is as empty as you might guess, except for a few condiments and some beer. Neither Mikey nor Joe (when he's there) is big on cooking, it would seem.

"What does your dad eat?" I asked Mikey one afternoon in the hangar, hoping perhaps to score some brownie points by showing up that night with Joe's favourite meal.

"He's the ultimate scrounger," he replied. "He picks at this and that. I don't think I've ever seen him cook. He's got a couple restaurants in town that cook for him. That's about it." Mikey's response should come as no surprise. The way I see Joe, he's too old-fashioned to cook for himself, and too busy to take the time, anyway.

CHANGE, IT SEEMS, is inevitable. Though I was proud of the magazines I produced as editor of *Up Here,* my time at the magazine was tumultuous. The corporate culture of the place seemed built around adrenaline, and my laid-back style was clearly a square-peg-in-a-round-hole scenario.

While I was there, I commissioned a writer to put together a piece about the perils and pitfalls of performing one's daily constitutionals, so to speak, in the wilds of northern Canada, an undertaking rife with such unexpected challenges as mosquitoes, flesh-freezing cold, and predatory mammals. I was planning on calling it "The Process of Elimination." To me, it was sheer brilliance; my bosses thought differently and I ended up leaving the magazine soon after that.

It would be months before Marty, Dawson, and I left Yellowknife for the mountain town of Canmore, Alberta, but the time was not without its milestones. As I began to navigate the murky waters of freelance writing and editing, we received news that baby Teya (named after Mary Teya, a highly respected elder from Fort McPherson) would soon be joining her brother Dawson as part of our family.

DESPITE ITS ADHERENCE to times past, Buffalo Airways is not immune to the forces of change, either. And of all the changes the company has had to make over the years, perhaps the most significant is how it gets fuel.

Buffalo's old piston pounders use a type of fuel called "avgas," short for aviation gasoline. Mikey figures Buffalo may be the biggest consumer of the stuff in North America, maybe the world. One of the issues with avgas is that it uses a toxic substance called tetra-ethyl lead (TEL) to improve its combustion stability. Although there are environmental concerns about the use of leaded avgas, it is still used widely around the world and is relatively easy to find. Everywhere except in remote northern outposts, that is. So while Mikey has no problem getting enough fuel to power his planes on the way out of Yellowknife, getting them home from remote communities that no longer stock avgas is another story.

"It's a political issue with avgas too, because it's leaded fuel," Mikey says. "A politician could say 'Hey, I'm gonna be the guy who took leaded gas away.' To an uninformed person, that seems great: no more leaded fuel. But we're talking about a half percent of all the aviation fuel burned on Earth. Meanwhile, the jet that flies that guy around during his campaign is blowing

Electra Facts & Figures

- CAPACITY: Five crew (three flight deck) and 98 passengers
- PRODUCTION: 170
- LENGTH: 31.85 metres (104 feet, 6 inches)
- WINGSPAN: 30.18 metres (99 feet)
- HEIGHT: 10 metres (32 feet 10 inches)
- MAXIMUM SPEED: 721 km/h (448 MPH) at 3,660 metres (12,000 feet)
- CRUISE SPEED: 600 km/h (373 MPH)
- RANGE: 3,540 kilometres (2,200 miles) with maximum payload 4,455 kilometres (2,770 miles) with 7,938 kilograms (17,500 pounds) payload
- EMPTY WEIGHT: 26,036 kilograms (57,400 pounds)
- MAXIMUM TAKEOFF WEIGHT: 51,256 kilograms (113,000 pounds)

way more hydrocarbons in the air than a DC-3 ever will. A 747 flying over here on its way to Tokyo is going to burn more fuel than a DC-3 will burn in a *month*. It's insane."

From what I can figure, a 747 burns 2,500 to 3,500 pounds of fuel every hour. Depending on the model, the plane carries from about 50,000 to 60,000 gallons, most of which it will use on an intercontinental flight. Ouch.

"So the real environmental issue is not in the name, but the quantity used." While I can see Mikey's point, I think he may be oversimplifying the issue, since studies conducted in the 1970s demonstrated the harmful effects of leaded gas combustion on people, especially children.

Either way, Buffalo's planes no longer have the luxury of flying from Point A to Point B, refuelling, and flying back home to Yellowknife, Mikey has started to find ways to maximize

Buffalo Airways' efficiency. He now schedules planes according to how far they can travel without having to carry extra fuel on board for the trip home. The DC-3 is most efficient for trips of about 400 kilometres (250 miles), maximum, compared with 900 kilometres (560 miles) for the C-46 and 1,300 kilometres (800 miles) for the DC-4. Back in the day, Buffalo planes would haul anything anywhere, because they didn't have to worry about how they would get back home. That's no longer the case.

"The reason we can't get leaded avgas fuel in the Arctic is supply and demand, simple Economics 101," Mikey says. "Nobody else uses it, so why would they bring it in?"

"Every time I book a charter now," he continues, "fuel is my biggest problem. Not pilots, not if the airplane is serviceable or not, and not which airplane to use. It's where am I going to get fuel?"

Although the bigger airports in the north still stock avgas, most of the smaller Arctic settlements stock ample supply of kerosene- or naphtha-based jet fuel, which is designed for use in aircraft powered by gas-turbine engines. That leaves out most of Mikey's fleet. Most, but not all. Enter the Electra.

THE LOCKHEED L-188 ELECTRA is like nothing else in the Buffalo fleet, for a number of reasons. To this casual observer, it seems harsher, more insensitive, colder. I know that sounds a bit crazy. After all, we're talking about machines. But the other planes in the Buffalo fleet all have a stately, almost regal air about them that you feel as soon as you are in their presence. There's a melancholy steeped into their very materials that whispers secret songs of lonely flights over mountain passes, lives lost far too young, and dreams dawning with the new day.

The Electra doesn't share that melancholy. To the extent that inanimate objects can be gendered, the Electra is all man. His props are hard, square, and harsh. His fuselage is sleek, businesslike. If planes could talk, the Electra would say "Let's get to work, I have shit to do," then glare at you if you offered it a cup of coffee.

When it was built, the Electra was the Hummer of the aircraft world. Its most macho characteristic was brute strength. The plane was powered by four high-performance turboprop engines that could help the plane take off and land on very short runways, meaning it had STOL (short takeoff and landing) capabilities. The engines use a gas turbine—the same kind of turbine that creates propulsion in jet engines—to drive their propellers, each generating 3,750 horsepower.

The plane was introduced in 1957 to a huge amount of fanfare as the first turboprop plane ever produced in the United States. The hullabaloo was short-lived. Not long after its introduction, the Electra was involved in three famous crashes in the fourteen months between February 1959 and March 1960. Order cancellations followed, bringing production to a halt.

With good reason. In two of the crashes, the Electra broke up in flight, which disturbed airlines about to spend millions of dollars on the aircraft. On September 29, 1959, Braniff Flight 542 crashed in Buffalo, Texas, en route to Dallas. All twenty-nine passengers and five crew members died. Less than six months later—on March 17, 1960—Northwest Orient Flight 710 broke apart in flight between Chicago and Miami, killing all sixty-three people on board.

It was later determined that both of those crashes were caused by something called a "whirl mode," which happens when a faulty engine creates a harmonic vibration so powerful that it rips a wing off a plane. Those structural problems have since been overcome, but the Electra's days were numbered before they really even started.

THE ELECTRA WAS also doomed by circumstance. Given its initial problems, the plane was sent back to the drawing board to have its engine mount fixed. In the meantime, Boeing introduced the Boeing 707, one of the first—and most successful—of the early commercial jets. Most of the world's major airlines passed over the Electra for the 707.

With few options remaining in the public sector, Lockheed sought refuge for the Electra and its variants in military and non-passenger use. A variant of the Electra, the P-3 Orion, has become one of the most successful planes ever built by Lockheed.

For Buffalo, the Electra is a perfect fit: it's older and less expensive than modern-day aircraft, but just as capable at moving tons of cargo from origin to destination. Rod McBryan agrees: it flies well, functions wells in the extreme arctic weather, and it's versatile. And perhaps most importantly, it burns jet fuel. Joe, the piston-engine diehard, struggled at first with the idea of the Electra, but he has since come to recognize the value the plane adds to Buffalo's business model.

For Justin, the Electra is a touch more complicated than the other planes. "An airplane is an airplane," he said through his cigarette smoke as we drove through Yellowknife in his hard-living Jeep Wrangler. "Ultimately they're all the same. But I would say the Electra is our most complicated airplane. Therefore, everything from its actual systems to what we've put together for a training syllabus is more complicated."

I can understand what they're both saying. Other than the Electra, Buffalo flies piston-pounding internal combustion engines. The company's expertise and skill is nested there, not with gas turbine engines. And while you may be thinking "an engine's an engine," nothing could be further from the truth. Asking a DC-3 mechanic to work on the Electra without the proper training is like asking a heart surgeon to operate on your brain. Couple that difference with the Electra's hyper-complicated electrical system, and you can see why Joe has to go out of his way to bring in Electra engineers to work almost exclusively on that plane.

"The Electra is a bit of a stretch for us," Mikey told me, "but we brought it in because we can't get avgas fuel in the High Arctic."

Complications notwithstanding, the Electra fits Buffalo's needs. It is an absolute beast when it comes to payload. The plane can hold as much as 15,000 kilograms (33,000 pounds) of cargo, good news for the people of the outlying communities who depend on Buffalo to keep them fed, clothed, and warm. And while all this cargo loading and delivery may mean big dollars for Buffalo, it translates to big stress for the woman who keeps the proverbial ship afloat when it comes to organizing, managing, and distributing the company's wares: cargo manager Kelly Jurasevich.

Thankless job? Perhaps. But Kelly handles her professional responsibilities kindly and efficiently. She gets the job done, and somehow manages to keep people as happy as possible at times when humour seems in short supply.

Kelly is primarily responsible for sending food and hard goods to Déline, Tulita, Norman Wells, and Fort Good Hope. Without Kelly, the stores in those towns (each has two stores, typically a Northern store and a Co-Op) would have bare shelves. On a typical shipping day, Kelly organizes and prioritizes about 40,000 kilograms (88,000 pounds) of goods, a phenomenon that occurs at least twice every week. The flight plan she concocts decides which store gets what, and when.

"You can't give everything to everyone at the same time," she told me in the Buffalo offices one day. "So I know who to not piss off, who I can bump, and who I can't. If I don't get those potato chips to Seymour at Great Bear Co-Op, is he ever pissed!"

She swears like a trucker (hell, she was one!) and smokes like a chimney, but Kelly Jurasevich is one of the warmest people you'll ever have the pleasure of meeting. She's also the heart and soul of Buffalo's cargo operations up the Mackenzie Valley.

Add the weather vagaries, and you can see how stress is Kelly's constant companion. "In the summer you gotta make sure the frozen stuff doesn't thaw, and in the winter you gotta make sure the perishables don't freeze. It can be really draining."

KELLY MAY BE DRAINED by her professional responsibilities, but she's the kind of person who always reserves a lot for the people in her life. The instant I met her, I knew she had one of those rare personalities that draws people to them. Kelly's smile lights up her face, the hearts of those around her, the rooms she walks into. Like so many who have been lucky enough to meet this woman, I immediately felt like she was my friend.

To listen to Kelly's life story is also an unbelievable experience. She smokes like a chimney and swears like a trucker. At the same time, she is the most lovable, mothering person you could ever hope to meet. And how she came to live in Yellowknife with her husband, Juan Trescher, is a tale that the finest fiction writers could not imagine.

With a case of Molson Canadian, Kelly and Juan's favourite beer, sitting on the counter, we dove into a couple of Caesars one late afternoon, the sun filtering through the windows of the mobile home she and Juan share. Drinking, I came to realize, is as much a fact of life in Yellowknife as swearing. Luckily, I'm okay with both.

Kelly was born the youngest of four children in Innisfail, a central Alberta town of around seven thousand people just south of Red Deer. When she was only seven years old, her mother succumbed to cancer; seven years later, her father died from alcoholism-related complications, sending Kelly on a journey that saw her enter foster care, live in a home full of bikers, marry a man who tried to kill her several times, move to Oregon for a second marriage, and then move to rural Vancouver Island, where she "hooked up" with Juan, to whom she's been married for thirteen years.

Kelly's road to the North started when Juan found himself out of work on Vancouver Island and received word of a possible opportunity: Buffalo Airways, a unique airline operating out of Yellowknife, Northwest Territories, needed a flight engineer on the Electra. Juan, who happened to be an Electra flight engineer, jumped at the job. Kelly had little interest in moving to a place she considered the end of the Earth. She wasn't counting on being sucked into the Buffalo vortex.

One day Rod McBryan asked Juan what kind of work Kelly did. "So I go in and they drag me into cargo," she recalls. "And all of a sudden they're showing me around like I have this job. I don't know an airport code from a hole in the wall. All of a sudden they're like, 'Oh, you got the job, Kelly.' *What* job?"

To make matters worse, Kelly's boss quit two weeks later, leaving Kelly to figure out Buffalo's cargo system on her own. Luckily, a few other Buffalo staff pitched in during the transition, though that didn't prevent Kelly from getting well acquainted with a bedfellow she has had ever since: stress. "I didn't sleep for about six fucking months," she says. "I cried myself to sleep every night."

Things didn't go particularly smoothly for Juan either. Like most employees, he had his predictable run-ins with Joe's temper. But Juan was not one to stand idly by when he felt wrongly attacked. So one day he told Joe what was on his mind, and quit. Juan is now a flight engineer for neighbouring First Air, working on the biggest cargo plane in the North: the L382G Hercules.

Kelly is still at Buffalo and has since mastered the nuances of her job, though that doesn't mean she loves it. Yet as much as she bitches and moans about her life in Yellowknife and dreams about living on a farm in Alberta, Kelly is quick to change her tune when she starts talking about the people she works with. From the rampies who seek her out for some motherly advice, to the store managers living in small communities along the Mackenzie River, Kelly lives for people.

"In our world today, everyone takes everything for granted. Nobody gives two shits about other people. And I was taught to do unto others as you want done unto you. My dad died in my arms when I was fourteen. And I had a hard fucking life. But I love what he instilled in me, and I will do that until the day I die. And I don't care if I ever get anything back, but I know I want to help people."

That's why when someone at Buffalo has a problem, Kelly gets the call. She knows when the rampies have been hurt by yet another scathing attack from Joe or someone else above them in the Buffalo food chain. That's when she calls them into her office and gives them a hug, a drink, or just a safe place to break down and cry.

"I will never push them aside because I'm too busy," she says. "It's what you have to do. Life is way too goddamn short." For Kelly, life is not about trips, toys, or material distractions. That outlook likely came at the hands of her great-grandmother Annie, with whom Kelly had an inseparable bond as a young girl. Annie taught her that life was a simple undertaking: focus on kindness and caring, and the rest will come. For Kelly, Annie's life had a wholesomeness about it that is difficult to match in today's world.

"That woman taught me everything I know," she recalls with a fondness that's palpable even through the blue haze of cigarette smoke hanging in the air between us and an ever-growing mountain of empty Canadians. "How to can, and how to cook. She taught me about the purity and simplicity of life."

Of the myriad stories Kelly goes on to tell me about Annie through the deepening—and ever drunker—night, there is one I'll never forget. Annie's husband Jacques was a hangman in Scotland who wanted to make a better life for himself in North America. So Jacques decided to take a boat ride across the Atlantic on a ship called the *Titanic*. With a few hours to go before the ship departed, Jacques decided to visit a local pub to help pass the time. "He got so fuckin' drunk he missed the boat!" Kelly said in a roar of laughter.

With that, we bid farewell to one another. The night had turned dark and cold, the hour was late, and Kelly had to be up in fewer hours than I cared to admit. As I settled into the cab, my arms full of Kelly's home-canned pickles, beets, and heirloom tomatoes, I fell asleep knowing that Buffalo's Yellowknife-based cargo operation was in good hands.

8

A BUSH PILOT IS BORN

No matter where you are in the North—from the glacier-scoured hills of Baffin Island to the spruce forests of the Mackenzie River Valley—spring is a glorious time. Yellowknife is no different. The long, dark, cold, and lonely days of winter slowly start to ease their vise-like grip on the land—and on your heart. The black of darkness gives way to grey. Then, with a sudden rush, the golden glow of sunshine charges across the land, and light dominates the days and nights. Believe it or not, warmth soon follows.

For my young family back in the mid-1990s, spring was a time to enjoy those things that the cold had prevented us from doing all winter. We played outside, went for long walks around local lakes, and—when luck was on our side and we actually

had access to a vehicle—went farther afield and took day trips down the Ingraham Trail, a sixty-five-kilometre (forty-mile) road to nowhere that extends east of Yellowknife.

By April, life at Buffalo Airways had become second nature for me. I was learning the ins and outs of the ramp, knew the hangar and surrounding offices like the back of my hand, and had managed to form relationships with just about everyone who worked for the airline. With one glaring exception, that is. For all my work, charm, and perseverance, one thing continued to evade me: Joe's story.

Joe's story.

Joe's story. JOE'S STORY. JOE'S STORY.

Every time I set foot in the Buffalo hangar, the words cycled through my head like a message on a Times Square billboard. I may have flown in a DC-3 high over Great Slave Lake and chugged Coronas and Dos Equis with Mikey, but what haunted my very being was Joe's story—or, more precisely, the fact that Joe didn't seem particularly interested in *sharing* his story (or any story, for that matter) with me.

To the contrary, during the time I'd spent in Yellowknife, Joe had seemed increasingly disinterested in my existence, let alone in spending any time with me, opening up to me, becoming friends with me. Maybe he considered me much like he considers new rampies: he doesn't figure he needs to talk to them until he's seen them around for a while, in case they quit in the interim— which many do. "There's always one coming and another one leaving," he told me once, in a rare conversation.

If Joe would barely talk to me, that didn't stop almost everyone else I met from talking *about* Joe with me. No matter what the topic of conversation, eventually we ended up discussing Buffalo Joe McBryan. And more often than not, those conversations evolved into discussions about Joe's two very different sides. Joe is cranky. Joe is impossible to please. Joe is unreasonable, stubborn, pig-headed, and sometimes downright mean. Then there's the part of Joe that is less obvious, but no less talked about by those who have spent any amount of time with him. Joe is kind. Joe is generous. Joe is loyal. Joe is loving, thoughtful, and considerate.

And if there's anybody on the planet who can speak to the paradox of Joe, it's his wife of forty-five years, Sharon.

Sharon is so soft-spoken and demure that it's almost difficult to hear her speak. Yet there's a gleam in her eye that tells me she's got a feisty side too. It's little wonder. You don't last in a relationship with Buffalo Joe McBryan for more than four decades unless you've got a tough side.

Like Joe's, the chronology of Sharon's life revolves around the North. She was born in High Prairie, a small town in northern Alberta. When Sharon was twelve years old, her father took a job in Fort Smith, another small town perched on the border between Alberta and the Northwest Territories, but a few years later her father moved the family back to High Prairie. Once there, Sharon found the curriculum very different from what she had grown to love in Fort Smith.

"I ended up quitting high school and going back," she said to me one spring afternoon in the confines of the quiet conference room we had ducked into. "I had an aunt and uncle in Hay River, so I went to live with them." She worked as a teleprinter operator and soon met Joe. The year was 1964. Two years later, on February 5, 1966, they married.

Their anniversary had recently passed, so I asked Sharon the question burning in my mind: did Joe take her out for dinner or buy her flowers on the big day?

Sophie is a fixture in the Buffalo hangar, and a very important part of Buffalo Joe's life. He will often disappear with her for hours at a time, though nobody really seems to know where the boss takes his beloved mutt.

"Are you kidding? We've never celebrated an anniversary! I've always thought it would be the last one," she joked. "So for forty-five years it never happened."

Sharon could tell that I was beginning to believe the portrayal of Joe as a cold-hearted son of a bitch, so she stopped me. "Oh, he's pretty cozy when he wants to be. He's got a heart of gold."

You don't need to dig deep to find evidence of Joe's heart everywhere he goes. Peter Magill, the manager of Buffalo Airwear, was the first to give me a clue. Peter was hired by Mikey to run the store, and as such had never met Joe, but had heard—and seen—lots about him. So when Peter showed up for his first day on the job, he was naturally expecting Mikey to show him the ropes. No such luck: Mikey was off in Vancouver doing promotions for *Ice Pilots*. The first person Peter ran into?

Joe himself. Luckily for Peter, his introduction to the big boss went a little more smoothly than mine did.

"I figured he was a hard-ass because of what I had seen on the show," Peter told me one day as we sifted through mountains of new items destined for the store's shelves. "I came in with my dog, and Joe was doing dishes in the kitchen. Well, we start talking, and forty-five minutes later we're still chit-chatting. That's when I thought that what's being represented on the TV show is really not the man himself."

Maybe I should have brought my dog with me the first time I visited Buffalo. A chow mix rescued after the hurricane of the same name devastated New Orleans in 2005, Katrina's big brown eyes will warm anyone's heart, and Joe's love of furry four-legged creatures is legendary. Sick pets always fly for free between Hay River and Yellowknife to see the vet. "The SPCA in Hay River probably owes a good chunk of its existence to Joe," Peter said.

Dogs are a constant in the fabric of life at Buffalo Airways. Sophie—Joe's beloved mutt—is legendary around these parts, and seems to have free reign over the hangar and the tarmac. No matter where you're walking, thirteen-year-old Sophie is there, wandering over for a scratch on her bony rear.

In fact, of all the aviation memorabilia peppering the walls of the Buffalo offices—and there is plenty—my favourite item is a framed letter from Transport Canada addressed to Joe, dated May 23, 2000. The letter, from aviation enforcement inspector Dan Stelman, informs Joe that Mr. Stelman will be investigating an apparent violation of section 302.10(i) of the Canadian Aviation Regulations. Apparently Joe's dog was seen running across Runway 27 of the Yellowknife Airport on April 25, 2000.

For Inuit who still run dog teams, little has changed since this photo was taken in 1958. Inuit sled dogs are legendary for their strength and stamina, and in decades past were an integral part of northern life.

How bothered was Joe by the investigation? Affixed to a blank corner of the letter is a picture of Sophie, sitting in the captain's seat of a DC-3, her head hanging playfully out the window.

Sophie isn't the only dog in the Buffalo family. On my first day at the hangar, I ran into Hunter, Kelly Jurasevich's salt-and-pepper border collie. Kelly was away on a vacation with Juan, and a member of the TV crew agreed to watch Hunter. Yet it was Joe who lavished the most attention on Kelly's dog, and certainly not just while Kelly was away. Hunter was later killed in an accident, which devastated Kelly—and, I imagine, Joe as well.

"Joe loved my dog," she told me one morning over donuts and a smoke. "He came to cargo every day, would do this funny whistle and call for Hunter. All of a sudden the two of them would hop in Joe's truck and off they would go. And to this day I don't know where he ever took him. But he always had Hunter, and he was good to my dog."

Sometimes, though, members of the Buffalo team struggle to see Joe treat animals so kindly while they bear the brunt of his temper. "I'll never forget one time I was irritated at work and Joe comes to get Hunter," Kelly recalled. "I yelled out, 'I wish I was a dog.' Well, he was kinda grumpy that day, and glares and me and says 'What the hell is that supposed to mean?' and just drives away.

"Sometimes you get treated better as a dog around here than as an employee."

OUR CONVERSATION reminded me of an experience I had when I lived on Baffin Island in the nineties, a time in my life that afforded me the opportunity to see and do things I had never imagined in my former, big-city-boy life. Chief among these was the chance to spend the day with my Inuit friend Esa Paniloo (not his real name), who asked me if I wanted to join him and his dog team out on Baffin Bay to check his nets. Esa set nets under the sea ice throughout the winter to catch fish and seals, thereby providing food for his family and his dogs. He checked his nets at least once a week, and thought I would enjoy the trip.

It was –40° the morning we headed out, so I donned every piece of warm clothing in my wardrobe. Before long, we were skimming along the undulating snow and then the ice, with nothing but the soft patter of the dogs' paws to accompany the most profound solitude I've ever known.

And while the cold was deep and frightening, we found moments of respite when our body weight was too much for the dogs and we had to run alongside the sled. That was when we warmed up, and quickly too.

At one point we stopped for tea and lunch, and I wasn't surprised to find that my peanut butter and jam sandwich now boasted the consistency of a hockey puck. A bigger shock came when I realized I had to pee, an undertaking that required a fair bit of bravery in the teeth of –40° temperatures. The prospect of frostbite is unattractive no matter where it might strike, but certain body parts were never meant to feel that kind of pain.

As we sat there, enjoying the infinite glory of a brilliantly clear Arctic day, the dogs decided they had had enough lounging around and took off with the sled, leaving us an uncomfortable distance from town with only our feet to get us back. Esa did the one-kilometre Arctic sprint, though, and eventually caught his renegade dog team.

Having been raised in a dogs-as-pets society, I thought this was all in good fun. Esa—who was brought up in a culture where dogs were tools—didn't see things the same way. After he caught them, he beat them. Badly. I remember clearly how he

Red McBryan, First Mayor of Hay River

WHEN I first visited Buffalo in January 2011, Joe visited nightly with his mother, Bertha, and father, Wilson Roderick (a.k.a. "Red"), both in their nineties. Red McBryan—the first mayor of Hay River—died on June 30, 2011, at the age of ninety-two.

Named for the colour of his hair, Red was born on April 26, 1919, and as a youth dreamed of moving to Aklavik, a small community in the Mackenzie River delta. Those dreams came true in his teen years, when he worked as a deckhand on a trading ship in the area. From there he moved to Yellowknife, where he worked at the Giant Mine and met Bertha. They moved to Hay River in 1949, where Red became actively involved in local politics. He became the town's first mayor in 1963 and served as a town councillor for forty-nine consecutive years between 1952 and 2000.

Joe was one of the people who spoke at his dad's funeral.

"We could not say goodbye to Red McBryan, or who we called Dad," he said, "because to say goodbye is to say goodbye to ourselves. So we will not say goodbye, we will instead say thank you."

put the lead dog—a massive, powerful beast—in a headlock and punched it in the head over and over again.

It was the kind of thing I would have frowned upon in my former life, where dogs fit neatly in your lap and wore cute little sweaters. In this world, though, the possibility of being stranded out on Baffin Bay with nothing but the clothes on our backs was so acutely real that it was almost painful.

"I don't like disciplining them," Esa said, "but they have to know they can't do that."

Later, as we headed home in the purple haze of Arctic twilight, I realized that the stark reality of the North is what makes people here so quick to smile and say hello. It took a while to get used to, but I eventually came to realize that friendliness is one of the North's greatest natural resources. Don't bother knocking, just come right in. The tea's over there, help yourself. And as I would soon discover, Joe McBryan can demonstrate that northern friendliness too. It's just that his soft side is a little more elusive than his hardened shell.

That's why you can't really blame the TV crew for focusing on Joe's, um, *difficult* side. If you're in the hangar, you know when Joe is on a rampage because you can hear it, feel it in the air. Joe's soft side is, well, softer. So unless you're right there with a camera, you're going to miss it.

But with time, however, Joe's portrayal on the show has become mellower. And I don't think that's because Joe himself changed fundamentally. Rather, the team behind *Ice Pilots* has come to recognize that there's more to Joe than meets the eye.

Joe flies to Yellowknife every morning, then spends his day in mysterious ways. Nobody, it seems, knows what he does between landing at 8:30 AM and taking off again at 5:00 PM (4:30 PM on Sundays), though taking dogs to unknown destinations is clearly part of it. "I can guarantee you he's thinking about fifteen different things, though," Mikey told me.

When Joe gets back home to Hay River every night, he follows the same routine: he goes to his mother and father's house for a visit before returning to his own home on the banks of the Hay River, and Sharon.

"THAT'S JOE'S OLD-SCHOOL NATURE," says Peter, who also lives in Hay River, commuting back and forth with Joe on the DC-3 every morning and evening. "How many people do you know who visit their mom and dad every night? It touched my heart, actually."

Joe's ephemeral kind streak is not only reserved for four-legged creatures or his parents, though. Almost everywhere you go in Yellowknife, someone has a story about Joe helping him or her out of a dire situation. Peter Magill tells of a Hay River family whose son was tragically killed in a car accident in Edmonton. Without a second thought, Joe fired up his five-passenger Beechcraft Baron and flew to Cambridge Bay, some 850 kilometres (525 miles) to the north, to retrieve some of the family members and bring them back to Hay River for the funeral.

"There's a thread of humanity that runs through this company," Peter said.

Too true. On one of my forays through the Pilots' Lounge I met pilot Rob Zonneveld, a delight of a man who has been in Yellowknife for ten years, though not always with Buffalo. Rob's story is a little different from most. After paying his dues on the Buffalo ramp and getting checked out on the DC-3, Rob was almost immediately promoted to flying the CL-215 water bomber to help fight fires during the summer season.

After four years with Buffalo, though, Rob decided to accept an offer from neighbouring Arctic Sunwest Charters. Then the recession hit and Arctic Sunwest stopped flying the de Havilland DHC-5 Buffalo, the plane Rob had been flying while there. "So I went back to Joe and asked for my job back," he told me.

Given what I've heard and seen of Joe, I couldn't imagine that would have been a comfortable situation for Rob. I could picture Joe wielding his power like an iron fist, bringing it down on Rob's unsuspecting skull in one fell swoop.

"So, did Joe hold it against you?" I asked.

"Hold it against me?" Rob scoffed. "When I came back it was like the prodigal son returning. I thought he was going to go kill his seven strongest bison and hold a feast. It was an awesome experience; felt like I was coming back to family."

That's not the only time Joe's kindness has surprised Rob. As a young rampie struggling to survive in one of the world's most expensive towns, Rob woke up one morning to find that his tires—along with those of most others on his street—had been slashed during the night.

"I was bitching about it to the boys, and Joe must have overheard me talking. So he walked me out to the backyard, where he's got a bunch of old cars laying around. And he told me to find tires that fit my car and take them. They didn't really match and they were a bit wide, but they got on the vehicle and away I went. It saved me a couple hundred bucks, which was a really big deal at the time.

"So he's definitely sensitive to a person's experiences. But at the same time, when it's time to work, it's time to work."

Work. For Joe McBryan, it's always time to work. Indeed, the words "work" and "Joe McBryan" seem synonymous. Working hard is a trait that has apparently been passed on to his children. I wonder how Joe would react to the "Live More, Play More" attitude that defines my current home of Canmore, Alberta, where ten centimetres (four inches) of snowfall sees school kids come down with the "powder flu" and go skiing, and a sunny day is an excuse for hitting the mountain bike trails. If Canmore had a town slogan, it would have to be the one espoused by my good friend Ben Waldman: work is for losers.

Given the disparate cultures of Canmore and the Buffalo hangar, I chose to keep my love of recreation to myself when in Joe's company—or anyone else's company, for that matter.

It's hard enough being an outsider. I didn't need to further hamstring myself by throwing in the fact that I love to play too.

I WAS IN the hangar one Sunday morning, and the place was deserted. For the first time I could remember, the inside of the massive, vaulted building was dead quiet. Nobody was yelling, and the sound of the banging of tools had been temporarily hushed. The planes stood watch over the place, silent sentinels resting before the next job took them afield. My footsteps echoed loudly through darkened corners. Even Sophie, who had become one of my closest allies in Yellowknife, had not wandered over to me.

Soon I was parked in the small kitchen off the hangar, taking notes, enjoying a cup of tea and shooting the shit with members of the T V team who had just arrived, when Joe walked in and seated himself in a threadbare chair beside me. Then, out of the blue, he started talking. Not bitching, not barking, not interrogating. Just talking.

Joe is talking!

And when Joe talks, you have to stay on your toes. It takes only a few seconds to realize that he's not one to linger on a word, sentence, or topic for long. The conversation is fast-paced, almost frenetic, as he jumps from year to year, location to location.

From what I can gather, Joe grew up as Wilson Claude McBryan in a bush camp on the shores of Gordon Lake, about 110 kilometres (70 miles) northeast of Yellowknife, where his father worked as a gold miner. "When he was born," Mikey once told me, "there were three new babies at the Yellowknife Hospital: a Joseph, a Josephine, and my dad. The nurses nicknamed him Joey, because there were already two other Joes there. And it stuck."

Once little Joe was old enough to go to school, he was sent off to Edmonton, where he lived with a grandmother. "I couldn't go to public school because my grandma paid taxes to a separate school board," Joe said, bouncing in and out of the kitchen from nearby offices. He was on a roll, speaking fast and moving faster. It was exhausting to listen to him, let alone to try to keep up with him. "So I had to go to a Catholic school. That was okay, see, because I was born a Catholic but didn't practise that shit."

That didn't stop Joe from knowing some choice words when he got to school: "Goddamn, Jesus Christ. That's what you said when you hit your thumb with the hammer!" Somehow, Joe was made an altar boy.

"The nuns had a lot of fun with changing me around. But I got to know those prayers pretty good. I couldn't sing, so they taught me Latin. I could say the whole mass in Latin, eh?"

Growing up in Edmonton without his parents wasn't always easy for Joe, especially when it came to the parochial world of sports. "There were lots and lots of rinks and baseball diamonds in Edmonton at the time," Joe said, feasting upon a breakfast of champions: handfuls of Big Turk candies and coffee. "If your dad wasn't part of the Knights of Columbus, you got no ice time or baseball time. I had nobody in the Knights of Columbus, so I wasn't picked or chosen or coached to the level I could have been. I could never find a coach to get me from being a bad skater or hitter to being a hockey player or baseball player."

The structured life of Edmonton was never a good fit for Joe, and he relished every chance he had to get back up north. Setback after setback proved that school was never in the cards for young McBryan. Joe spent the summer he was thirteen in Hay River, where his family had since moved after leaving Gordon Lake. Late one afternoon, Joe was sitting in the back of a pickup truck when it plummeted over a nine-metre (thirty-foot) cliff at a construction camp. Things did not look good; Joe had a broken pelvic bone and torn ligaments around his stomach, the nearest road was hundreds of kilometres away, and the sky was darkening.

Frantic, Joe's father, Red, called one of the few men he trusted enough to hand his injured son to: legendary bush pilot Chuck McAvoy, who would become one of the most important influences in Joe's life. McAvoy flew Joe to the Yellowknife hospital safely, carrying him into the waiting room wrapped in a sleeping bag "like a kid in a car seat." Joe credits McAvoy with saving his life that night. And Joe McBryan is not one to forget a good turn.

The accident slowed Joe's academic career in Edmonton to a crawl, however, as he was confined to a body cast for the better part of a year. Joe is still astonished when he thinks back on the time he lost, especially given the medical advances that have occurred in the interim.

"I had a friend hit by a truck down south," he says between pieces of Big Turk. "When I talked to his wife, she thought he was gonna die. Well, I phone back a couple days later to see how he's doing, and he answers the phone! I said, 'I thought you were dying!' "

By the end of that year, Joe had had enough. He quit school in Edmonton and headed back to Hay River, but the truant officer caught up with him and hauled him back. "They said, 'Ya gotta be in school until you're sixteen.' So I had to go back."

At sixteen, Joe was out again. "School is a good place to be if you like it," he said. "But it was not a good place for me." That should come as little surprise. How can school compete with the feeling of flying, which Joe was doing by the time he was in

Grade 10? "How do you fly and go to school at the same time?" Unable to reconcile that conundrum, Joe chose flying.

"Back then we considered ourselves the same as a kid on a tractor on a farm," he said. "The kid in the city can't drive worth shit at sixteen, but the kid on the farm is versatile on everything at ten. For us, there were no roads out of Hay River at that time, and airplanes were more common than cars. So we knew all about airplanes, just like kids in the city know all about buses and trains and subways or whatever." Not surprisingly, Joe saw an airplane long before he ever saw a car (the road north from Hay River to Yellowknife wasn't built until 1968).

That familiarity may have bred a certain level of comfort, confidence, and ability in the young McBryan, but others didn't always perceive him as competent. "When I was in Grade 10, I flew into Fort Liard [about 400 kilometres or 250 miles to the west] on a charter," he remembered. "There were no scheduled flights or airstrips back then, so when I arrived on the ice, everyone in town came out to see what was happening.

"Well, the town cop came out and looked at me and said, 'What the hell are you doing flying that fucking airplane? I wouldn't even give you a driver's licence last year and now you're flying that goddamn airplane?'"

Perhaps the RCMP officer was unaware of the fact that Joe had grown up in airplanes—literally. When he was just a small boy, a de Havilland Fox Moth crashed not far from the Gordon Lake camp the McBryans called home. Along with Chuck McAvoy, Joe's father went out with a team of nine dogs to the wreck site. "They stripped the plane of its engine and useful parts, and hauled it all back to camp," Joe said. The fuselage became his playhouse.

The Fox Moth served a purpose for the adults as well. "I needed a playhouse because they were always blasting for gold and had to get me out of the way. So they'd throw me in the airplane, pull the canopy shut and tell me to 'fly' to town for a load of groceries while they were blasting." To this day, the door of that fuselage hangs in Joe's Yellowknife office, one of a thousand pieces of memorabilia, tokens of a life well lived, that adorn the place.

Joe waxes nostalgic when he thinks back on those innocent days of his youth. But not everyone shares his opinion. "There used to be an old prospector in town here—he's dead now—and he was cranky beyond cranky. I'd see him getting his groceries sometimes, and if I had time, I'd always stop and talk to him.

"One day he says to me, 'You still at the airport fucking around with them airplanes?' " he said, using a high-pitched voice that hints the prospector resided firmly on the loonier side of the spectrum. "I says, 'Yeah.' And he says, 'Well, you're crazy, and I know why you're crazy.'

"And I says, 'Well, that's good. But if I'm crazy, you should tell me why I'm crazy.' And he says, 'Yeah, back when you were a little boy they'd take you and put you in than little airplane and they'd shut the canopy and go blast all day. No wonder you went crazy sitting in that plane all day!' "

Although I'm pretty certain that Joe's not crazy, I can attest to one thing: those early days playing in the Fox Moth set Joe down a path that has carved out a unique niche in Canadian aviation history. With Chuck as his mentor, Joe was an accomplished pilot before he was twenty years old.

But bureaucracy, it would seem, reared its head even back then, and eventually Joe was forced to get a pilot's licence, even though he had been flying for years. "At that time, we didn't

Willy Laserich's Last Battle

WILLY LASERICH fought Arctic weather and remoteness for decades, but his toughest battle came in the courtroom in the 1970s, after federal regulators began playing a more heavy-handed role in northern bush flying. Willy tried to play by the rules, applying for an operator's licence to run a charter air service out of Cambridge Bay, but he was repeatedly turned down. That didn't stop Willy: he continued flying.

In 1977, Willy was charged with 205 citations for breaking aviation laws, a process that kick-started one of the longest and most expensive aviation trials in Canadian history. In the end, Willy was cleared of all but one charge, which carried a $250 fine. But the legal fees left him bankrupt. Rather than give up, his family banded together and formed Adlair Aviation, with offices in Cambridge Bay and Yellowknife. Willie died on November 12, 2007. He was seventy-five.

learn to fly in flying school," he said. "We went to flying school for the theory, to learn how to pass the exam. But you learned to fly from the other guys. You flew with Chuck and you flew with Jimmy and you flew with Willy and you flew with Merlyn and you were taught to fly. Flying school was a formality." Joe's mentors are now considered the legends of northern bush flying: Willy "The Flying Bandit" Laserich, Merlyn Carter, and Chuck and Jimmy McAvoy.

WILLY LASERICH came by his nickname honestly, forging a reputation as a rule-breaking maverick who stuck thorns in the sides of aviation regulators every chance he got. A native German, Laserich moved to Hay River in 1960 with a fresh pilot's licence in one hand and a new bride in the other. There, Willy would take a young Joe McBryan out flying. Willy and Margaret called several communities home in their early northern years, eventually settling in Cambridge Bay, a remote Nunavut community of some fifteen hundred souls on Victoria Island in the Arctic Ocean.

Merlyn Carter may have operated on the right side of the law, but he was no less influential in building the landscape that forged young Joe McBryan's life. A Saskatchewan native, Merlyn got his pilot's licence in Hay River in 1952 to help his father run their new commercial fishery there. Ten years later, Merlyn and his wife, Jean, started Carter Air Services. All the while, Merlyn was always there to help a young pilot learn the finer points of flying.

To help pay the bills during those early, lean years of their new company, Merlyn set up a number of camps throughout the Northwest Territories, where he began taking fishermen. Those spots eventually developed into one main camp, which still operates, at Nonacho Lake, some 300 kilometres (185 miles) southeast of Yellowknife.

Merlyn's life came to a tragic end in June 2005, when a black bear mauled him to death on the shores of the lake that had been his home away from home for so many years. To this day, he is considered a pioneer of both bush flying and tourism in the North.

Though Merlyn certainly played a role in young Joe McBryan's life, it paled in comparison to the influence that Chuck and Jim McAvoy had on the budding bush pilot. In some ways, Jim McAvoy was everything his brother Chuck was not. Chuck was gregarious and loud, Jim quiet and reserved. Yet there was one thing that had Jim and Chuck joined together: they were both incredible pilots who made their mark on the early years of northern bush flying.

Both also had an uncanny knack for finding lost souls in the remote northern wilderness, regardless of what the authorities told them. In one famous incident in 1957, a plane with three people aboard was forced to land in the Gameti (then called Rae Lakes) area, about 240 kilometres (150 miles) northwest of Yellowknife. Authorities ordered McAvoy not to fly—it was too late in the season for float planes and too early for ski planes—but Jimmy went anyway, eventually rescuing the trio. That heroic effort saw him grounded for thirty days. McAvoy died on November 21, 2009, in Thorsby, Alberta, at the age of seventy-nine.

Nevertheless, Joe did learn things at flight school that his childhood heroes hadn't taught him: radio usage, flight planning, paperwork, and log books.

But the bureaucracy was not finished with Joe. What started then as an aggravating relationship has continued to this day. Don't expect Joe to be singing the praises of Transport Canada. His song has a slightly different refrain, one learned in those days of his youth. As he explained:

"I go get a student's pilot permit, but the permit says you can fly but not haul people. Well, I didn't want to haul people anyway, so that's good enough. But then Transport gets all over my ass and now I have to go off and get a private pilot's licence.

"Now I go get this private licence down in Edmonton. And I get back and I'm flying again, and they say 'No, your private licence is only good for 4,300 pounds gross takeoff weight, why are you flying this Norseman [7,000-pound gross takeoff weight]. So now I have to get a special endorsement on my private licence to fly the damn Norseman."

As far as Joe and his cronies were concerned, though, the piece of paper did not make someone a pilot. "You never carried it with you, anyway," he laughed, "because you could either fly or you couldn't. And if you couldn't fly, then get the hell outta here. And if you can fly, then the paper doesn't have any significance anyway."

By the time Joe was nineteen years old, he had to get a commercial pilot's licence, yet another stop in a seemingly endless bureaucratic chain of events. "Chuck said if I wanted to fly on his Fairchild 82, I had to get a commercial licence. So he hands me this little twenty-five-cent book he had and told me to learn everything in there and take the exam.

"So I roar off to Edmonton to get a commercial licence. Well, I blew that right off the bat. That little book was obsolete as shit." Undaunted, Joe took the exam again, this time with the proper study materials. He eventually returned north with a commercial pilot's licence in his pocket. That was June 4, 1961. Less than ten years later, Joe would be at the head of a fledgling airline struggling to make its presence felt in one of the world's last great frontiers. He couldn't have imagined then that he would be the focal point of books, TV shows, and websites.

But that's certainly no shortcoming on Joe's part, just a function of who—and what—he is. For at his heart, Joe is a bush pilot, and a damn good one at that. And bush pilots are a special breed. In some ways, they embody everything that Joe is, was, and may yet be. They're stubborn, pig-headed, entrepreneurial, rebellious, story-telling pioneers who live for the freedom of soaring above the clouds, unencumbered by worldly woes.

9

FLYING THE WILD

To be a bush pilot is to be an icon, a living mystery, an individual whose essence speaks of the tough, ready, creative, and self-sufficient stuff we all wish we were made of. In a country like Canada, the national identity is still strongly linked to wilderness, and bush pilots have played an important role in settling those far-flung northern regions that most people will never get to see.

Although the terms "bush flying" and "bush pilots" have become inextricably linked with northern Canada and Alaska, the term likely originates from southern Africa, where the word "bush" was used to describe the land there. Since then, its meaning has expanded to include any remote wilderness area; hence its attachment to two of the wildest places left on the planet. Bush flying is still widely practised in Australia as well.

"Bush flying" refers to flying aircraft in these sometimes-inhospitable regions. Conditions such as extreme and unpredictable weather, distance from civilization, and the roughness of the terrain all combine to make bush flying one of the most demanding—and dangerous—endeavours on the planet. In many instances, bush pilots do not have the luxury of landing their craft on prepared landing strips, let alone runways. That's why many of today's bush planes still ply northern skies equipped with floats, skis, or unusually large tires, sometimes called "tundra tires."

Bush flying was first used in eastern Canada as a way of exploring and developing otherwise unreachable parts of the country. By the end of World War I, most of southern Canada—that thread of land that lies close to the border with the United States—had been linked by railways. The North, however, remained as remote, wild, and inhospitable as it had ever been.

In late 1918, a Canadian forester named Ellwood Wilson had the idea of using aircraft to spot forest fires and map forested areas. A year later he managed to get his hands on a couple of Curtiss HS-2L flying boats, biplanes whose fuselages were shaped and sealed like the hull of a boat, allowing them to take off, land, and float on water. Soon thereafter, pilot Stuart Graham and engineer Walter Kahre were selected to fly the planes. On June 4, 1919, Graham and Kahre began a 1,038-kilometre (645-mile) journey to Lac-à-la-Tortue, Quebec, then the longest cross-country flight ever flown in Canada.

That summer, Graham (whom many consider to be Canada's first bush pilot) and Kahre performed aerial reconnaissance to spot forest fires in Quebec's St. Maurice River valley. Meanwhile, the Southern Labrador Pulp and Lumber Company of Boston hired pilots to perform extensive aerial surveys of lands the company leased in Labrador.

By the mid-1920s, bush flying had conquered the eastern Canadian winter as well, as a pilot named Doc Oaks, who flew supplies for a local mining company, developed methods to heat and maintain engines in Canada's brutal winter conditions. A pair of brothers from Sioux Lookout, Ontario, developed special skis that would land on snow or ice. Much of the flying during this era—as today—was in support of mining operations.

Flying for profit was a questionable undertaking back on the eve of the Great Depression. The early 1920s saw a serious decline in the number of licenced pilots, aircraft, and flying companies registered in Canada. By 1924, there were only eight private airlines left in the country. Yet as their numbers fell, their workloads grew: more than 77,000 pounds of cargo were carried in 1924, a huge increase from the 14,600 pounds carried in 1921.

Things turned around in 1924, when the Canadian Air Force decided to discontinue any flying operation that could instead be performed by a private company; commercial flight was reborn. The Ontario government was so convinced that aircraft would change the landscape of the country that it created the Ontario Provincial Air Service, which ultimately attracted some of the best pilots and engineers from around the country. Though the service's primary mandate was to fight fires, its pilots themselves performed a variety of jobs, including aerial photography, emergency medical flights, and land surveys.

The story was developing in much the same way in western Canada, where a young man named Wilfrid "Wop" May (he got his nickname from a young cousin who pronounced

Wilfrid as "Woppie") moved to Edmonton after his discharge from the Royal Naval Air Service. A Montreal businessman thankful for his success in Edmonton's booming real estate market had given the city a Curtiss JN-4 airplane as a token of his appreciation. May quickly asked if he could rent the plane, a request that was granted. Soon afterwards, May Airplanes—the first commercial bush-flying operation in western Canada—was created. One of May's first jobs was to fly copies of the *Edmonton Journal* to the town of Wetaskiwin, some 70 kilometres (45 miles) to the south.

October 1920 saw what may be Canada's first commercial bush flight into the untamed wild. A fur buyer walked into the downtown Winnipeg offices of Canadian Aircraft and asked to be flown home to the small town of The Pas, hundreds of kilometres to the north. By 1921, Imperial Oil was using a fleet of aircraft to explore the Northwest Territories, and got within 160 kilometres (100 miles) of the Arctic Circle.

Canada's airline industry changed forever when, in 1926, a wealthy Winnipeg grain merchant named James A. Richardson—who would go on to be called the father of Canadian aviation—formed Western Canada Airways. The airline served many purposes in those early years of aviation. One of its most astonishing trips involved a prospector named Gilbert LaBine and a pilot named Wilfred Leigh Brintnell. In 1929, LaBine and Brintnell set out from Winnipeg for Great Bear Lake, where LaBine was dropped off in search of precious metals. Brintnell then continued his journey north to Aklavik, across the Richardson Mountains (named for a different Richardson, Sir John) to Whitehorse, west to the northern B.C. town of Prince George, then back to Edmonton and finally to

In 1932, the Royal Canadian Mounted Police hired bush pilot Wilfrid "Wop" May to hunt the fugitive Albert Johnson, the "Mad Trapper of Rat River," from the air.

Winnipeg, a journey of some 15,000 kilometres (9,320 miles). The prospector LaBine would go on to strike it rich when he discovered pitchblende, a uranium-rich form of uraninite.

AMONG OTHER THINGS, the formation of Richardson's Western Canada Airways helped bring new aircraft into the Canadian fold. The company soon placed an order for twelve Fokker Universals from the United States. The Universal boasted radial, air-cooled engines designed and built by aviation manufacturer Pratt & Whitney. The Universal's design soon became the industry standard, a position it held until the early 1930s.

It wasn't long before those little Fokkers were making their mark on life in the bush. In one case, a New York businessman needed financial papers to be signed by a prospector living in the gold fields of remote northern Ontario. The telegram was sent from New York to Hudson, Ontario, the base of Western Canada Airways, where Doc Oaks then flew the telegram to Narrow River and snowshoed to the prospector's cabin. The two men then hiked back to the plane and flew to Sioux Lookout, where the prospector signed the papers at a local bank. A three-week expedition had been reduced to less than a day.

But the Fokkers were not without their shortcomings, which opened the door for other bush planes to fly through. In 1928, de Havilland Aircraft of Canada began assembling two-seater Gipsy Moths outside of Toronto. The Reid Aircraft Company was established at Montreal that same year; in 1929, the Fairchild Aviation Corporation built a large aircraft manufacturing plant in Montreal.

The creation of Canadian Airways—a merger between Richardson's Western Canada Airways with the Aviation

Corporation of Canada—in November 1930 continued the development of new planes. In 1931, Canadian Airways introduced the Junkers Ju 52 ("Iron Annie"), at that point the largest single-engine aircraft ever to grace Canadian skies. From the Yukon Territory to Quebec, the Ju 52 made a name for itself by the incredible amounts of freight it could carry.

Soon thereafter, the Fairchild Super 71 was introduced, the first aircraft ever designed in Canada for bush operations. It was followed by the Fairchild 82. In mid-1935, the first plane ever completely designed and built in Canada—the Noorduyn Norseman—rolled off the assembly line at the Noorduyn plant in Montreal. The Norseman was the quintessential Canadian bush plane. Fast, roomy, comfortable, and economical, it could operate on wheels, skis, or floats, and carried up to ten people. And as I would go on to learn late in the summer of 2011, the Norseman was such a good plane that it still flies today.

While the Norseman may have been the first bush plane built on Canadian soil, it is certainly not the only one to make its mark on the country's bush flying history. From the mid-1940s to early 1950s, de Havilland Canada developed and built a pair of planes that would become as important in plying the skies of the remote Canadian wilderness as any other: the DHC-2 Beaver and the DHC-3 Otter. The Beaver was characterized by a host of refinements that allowed it to operate in cold climates, including extremely short takeoff and landing capabilities. The Otter capitalized on the successful design of the Beaver, but made it significantly bigger. Both planes were so popular that they were further modified, into the Turbo Beaver (a turboprop-driven version of the Beaver) and the DHC-6 Twin Otter (an expanded, twin-engine version of the Otter). The

The Flying Knight of the Northland

HE was the bush pilot who went by many names. Aboriginals of the north dubbed him "Snow Eagle"; non-aboriginals called him "White Eagle." To the press, he was "the Flying Knight of the Northland." No matter what his nickname, Clennell Haggerston "Punch" Dickins (pictured on page 172) was a pioneer of northern aviation.

Born in Portage la Prairie, Manitoba, at the turn of the twentieth century, Punch fought with the Canadian armed forces in World War I, where he became a bomber pilot. When he returned in the early 1920s, he was one of the first pilots to join Western Canada Airways, one of the airlines credited with opening up the West and North to the age of aviation.

Punch played a huge role in charting the unmapped Barrenlands of the North, flying more than a million miles in his career, often in treacherous weather conditions, with unreliable navigation aids and few landing strips. In 1928, Dickins flew one of the first aerial surveys of Canada in a Fokker Super Universal. In January 1929 he delivered the first airmail to the Northwest Territories, stopping at ten communities between Waterways, Alberta, and Fort Simpson, Northwest Territories. In classic Punch fashion, he extended the trip to Aklavik, in the bargain becoming the first pilot to ever fly the entire length of the Mackenzie River.

Punch's final flight came after his death, in 1995, when his ashes were scattered by his son John along the Mackenzie River.

Beaver played such a huge role in Canadian aviation history that in 1987 the Canadian Engineering Centennial Board named it one of the most significant Canadian engineering achievements of the twentieth century.

Bush flying changed the way people thought about travel in Canada and the accessibility of the North. The North once stood as the last great untamed wilderness on Earth, and one that required superhuman effort and will (not to mention years) to conquer, but by the 1930s you could charter a plane

Bush pilot Wally Carrlon stands on the float of this 1936-built Noorduyn Norseman. CF-BAU was the second Norseman ever built. The plane was reported as damaged beyond repair in 1951.

and fly almost anywhere, anytime. With the establishment of fuel caches in long-forgotten places and the operation of planes on floats or skis, the northland's utter isolation had become a thing of the past. Whether you were a geologist or trapper, missionary or entrepreneur, the North was open to you.

As long as you had a good engineer on hand, that is.

FOR AS LONG as planes have been in the skies, pilots have received most, if not all, of the glory associated with flying. The movie *Catch Me If You Can* portrayed the commercial pilot as nothing short of a rock star, with hordes of giggling flight attendants in tow. Early bush flying was nothing like that, and relied heavily on the behind-the-scenes guys who kept the planes functional: the engineers.

Back then, flight engineers were mechanics, and their responsibilities were myriad. Imagine a 1920s-era plane floating on a mosquito-infested lake in the Northwest Territories, or worse yet, in the darkness and –40 temperatures of mid-winter. The engine won't start, your supply of food is limited, and you have no way of communicating with the outside world. You had two choices: start swimming, or make the plane airworthy again. The latter was the engineer's responsibility. Bush pilots relied heavily on their engineers to keep the planes in the air.

Not surprisingly, engineers were also charged with keeping their planes in good working order to make sure mishaps didn't happen in the first place, especially in winter, when the risk of mechanical failure increased substantially. So when a long day of flying drew to a close, the engineer's day was just beginning. He had to drain the oil from the engine and carry it to the nearest shelter, where it would be kept warm overnight to prevent freezing. The next morning, he would pour the warmed oil back into the engine, which was also being thawed out, usually from a fire pot placed underneath. If the engine refused to start, the oil was re-drained out and the process started anew.

Hardships such as these helped early aviators to discover that planes built for more hospitable climates were not perfectly suited for the rugged conditions of Canadian wilderness and winters. Ideally, a plane needed several characteristics to be bush-worthy. Most importantly, it needed to be able to take off and land in small spaces. The wings of a typical bush plane were on top of its fuselage, which helped prevent contact with any overgrowth in the landing area.

Bush planes also embraced what's called a tail-dragger wheel configuration, where two main wheels sit forward of the plane's centre of gravity and a smaller wheel supports the tail, leaving the plane sitting in a decidedly "uphill" slant. The tail-dragger configuration is more suited to the rough landing areas of the Canadian bush, because it increases the upward angle of the plane upon takeoff, landing, and taxi, which affords the propeller more clearance from the ground (and rocks, logs, bushes, and other things that might wreak havoc on it).

BUSH FLYING IN CANADA has certainly changed since those days. The country's northern reaches remain remote and inhospitable, though access has greatly increased. There are more gravel airstrips than ever before, so the need to land on water or the tundra is not quite as acute as it once was. As a result, the smaller, more mobile, and more versatile bush planes of the past—although still ubiquitous—are not as vital as they once were. With more developed airstrips, larger planes such as the DC-3 have become more common.

Given that change, one might assume that the number of bush pilots is dwindling too. And that may be true. I couldn't help but think that when it came to the classic Yellowknife bush pilot, well, there ain't that many around. Then I met Carl Clouter.

Truth be told, I had never heard of Carl Clouter until I went to Yellowknife. He is not one of those famous bush pilots whose names are spoken in hushed, reverential tones, like some of his contemporaries. But if ever there were a human being who embodied the essence of what a bush pilot dreams to be, it's Carl Clouter.

I was driving along Yellowknife's still-hard-packed and deadly slick roads on an unseasonably warm April day when I decided to look Carl up. Though we had never met, he invited me over right away. Carl's voice sings of bush piloting. There's an ease to it, a relaxed, hell-I-know-I-can-handle-just-about-anything-thrown-at-me quality that makes you feel comfortable right away.

"You just drive down to Weaver and Devore," he said, referencing the hardware, clothing, and trading company that is an Old Town Yellowknife institution, "make a right, drive out onto the ice and look for the yellow plane in front of my place."

Sure, no problem. Just make a right at Weaver and Devore, turn right, drive out onto the... onto the... We are *so* not in Kansas anymore.

Carl, it seems, counts himself among a vibrant population of Yellowknifers that prefers the waters of Great Slave Lake's Back Bay to the city streets. In other words, Carl is a houseboater, who lives off the grid in a small floating trailer that affords a waterfront view in every direction. When the lake is ice-free (as it is for a frightening few months a year), Carl's trailer bobs in the waters a few hundred metres from shore and is only accessible by boat. When the lake is frozen, though, getting to Carl's place is as simple as driving across the ice—which I do, albeit a little disconcertedly.

No matter how much experience you have doing it, driving on ice—solid ice, with nothing underneath but water—is an unsettling experience. I drove slowly... really slowly... even though the packed layer of snow sitting on top offered a modicum of traction.

In addition to thoughts of my vehicle sinking to the bottom of Great Slave Lake, the other thing that rattled my cage ever so slightly was the fact that there were no signs or lanes or lines on the road to guide me to my destination. Let's face it, driving is a structured undertaking. You drive on the right-hand side of the road, stay in your lane, obey the signs and traffic lights. But once I drove down what seemed to be the boat launch beside Weaver and Devore and out on to the open ice, structure went out the window. It was just me and the wide open spaces.

In all honesty, the freedom was a little frightening. Carl's house—frozen firmly in the metre-thick ice of Back Bay—was visible in the distance, the canary-yellow plane an obvious landmark, but I didn't know which way to go. Do I check right and left for passing dog teams? Will a snowmobiler give me the finger if I don't offer the right of way? Luckily, my fear was unfounded, if only for the simple fact that nobody else was driving on the road. So I did what came naturally: I drove straight for Carl's houseboat.

Engaging and quick to smile, and with a full mop of long, tousled grey hair that nearly covered his bushy salt-and-pepper eyebrows, Carl was at the door waiting when I pulled up, my shiny rental car a dead giveaway in a place where most vehicles boast that hardened look that speaks more to function than form—up here, vehicles bear the scrapes and bruises of driving on roads carved out of permafrost, where encounters with salt, rocks, and animals occur more commonly than Yellowknifers would like to think.

Before long, we were sitting inside Carl's cozy, wood-heated home. Canada has always had a distinct odour for me: the rich, earthy, and rustic smell of burning wood. I first noticed it while working as a volunteer in northern Ontario, and the smell was present in almost every small Canadian community I've lived in, except on Baffin Island, where trees are non-existent. Yet from Batchawana Bay to Fort McPherson, all I needed to do was walk down the street on a spring, fall, or winter day, and invariably I would smell woodsmoke. Say what you want about the environmental effects of burning wood, the scent is glorious.

Carl lit his pipe and the warm living room air thickened as the sweet smell of pipe smoke mingled with the scent of burning wood. I sat back in the couch and enveloped myself in the scene, as Carl, whose thick moustache quivered delightfully every time he spoke, began to weave tales of a life as a bush pilot, philosopher, miner, prospector, and entrepreneur.

A Gander, Newfoundland, native, Carl was already experienced in the left seat when he moved to Yellowknife in 1973 on a three-month contract to help out Jimmy McAvoy, who needed a new chief pilot for McAvoy Air Service. "Jimmy made it well worth my while to stay with him rather than go back to water bombing, so I stayed with him for twenty-three years," Carl said in his heavy Newfoundland accent.

By 1990, Carl had started his own company, Edzo Air, which primarily flew members of the Dogrib nation on charters between the hamlets in the area. At any time of the year, Carl and his Cessna 206 could be seen flying between Rae-Edzo, a pair of sister communities just north of Yellowknife, and Whatì (then called Lac La Martre), Gameti (Rae Lakes), and Wekweti (Snare Lakes), a trio of hamlets about 200 kilometres (125 miles) northwest of Yellowknife.

Like Buffalo Joe, sixty-eight-year-old Carl strikes me as one of those people who has managed to carve out a professional life for himself doing exactly what he was put on Earth to do: fly. "It's not a job," he said with a wry smile, "it's the greatest profession in the world."

Where Carl and Joe diverge, though, is in what they do when they're up in the air. While Joe seems to use flying as a way to cleanse his mind of his myriad responsibilities, Carl is always looking down from the air—at geological formations on the ground, that is. Carl is not only a pilot, but a prospector as well, two vocations that go hand in hand.

Just like some of the biggest gold strikes in history, Carl's discovery of his calling came serendipitously. "I did some geology courses," he told me through the cloud of blue smoke hanging in the air between us. "Back in Newfoundland, I flew with Noranda Exploration a lot. That's when I got my first rock hammer. Then I got some books, and here I am."

If that all sounds a little accidental, don't be fooled. Over the years, Carl has developed a knack for prospecting, and he remains one of Yellowknife's most prolific prospectors. Everywhere I turned in his crowded living room, stacks of geology books were fighting for space. His shelves and window sills are peppered with hundreds of rock samples, in every size, shape, hue, and texture imaginable. Some were dull and grey, and tweaked no dreams of riches in my brain; others gleamed with flecks of precious metals and spoke of vast riches stored under millions of tons of earth. The extent of Carl's collection should come as no surprise, given its owner's history: in the years he has been prospecting, Carl has staked over 350 claims around Great Slave Lake.

IN THE PROSPECTING GAME, most claims fizzle out—the area holds few minable resources, or no company is interested in the claim, or logistical challenges prevent profitable development of a mine. Every once in a while, though, a prospector hits the proverbial motherlode, and things take off. I'm not sure if Carl is in this latter category, but he was not ashamed to tell me that he's "done very well prospecting."

Indeed he has. Carl is currently one of the directors of Fortune Minerals, a public company that trades on the Toronto Stock Exchange. In 1995, Carl was flying his Cessna when he discovered a gold-cobalt-bismuth-copper deposit about 160 kilometres (100 miles) northwest of Yellowknife. That find has become the focal point of Fortune's northern mining efforts; the company estimates that the NICO deposit contains 760,000 ounces of gold, 61 million pounds of cobalt, and 77 million pounds of bismuth. Once the company gets the go-ahead from the Tlicho government, mining will begin in earnest.

The way Carl describes it, successful prospecting involves much more than throwing a dart at a map. His research begins with old geological maps of the area, which are available from the territorial government. He then turns to a more modern tool: Google Earth. "It's great!" he exclaimed. "You can actually see faults and systems on Google Earth."

If Carl finds an area that tweaks his keen imagination, he'll take the next step and investigate, first by plane, then by foot. It's a pattern he's been repeating for decades. "Years ago when I was flying fire patrols for the government, I'd have their firefighting map and my prospecting map on board at all times," he said. "And if I saw something interesting in the rock, I would put a little 'x' on my map, to come back and check it out later. So I'm getting paid to do the fire patrol—and I stayed on their lines, of course—but I'm prospecting too!"

Carl always seemed to find time for a bit of prospecting, no matter what the job or who the client. "Let's say I was flying back to Fort Rae from Snare Lakes with a local RCMP officer, doctor, dentist, or social services worker," he recalled. "I'd ask if they would be interested in stopping for an hour or two to prospect, and they always said 'Sure, Carl!' Their job would be over, and they'd get a chance to see things they'd never seen before while I got to do a bit of prospecting."

Prospecting only starts with aerial observation. If you want to see what the Earth holds, you have to get down on the ground and start chipping away at it with your rock hammer. Find something interesting, and the sample is sent to a lab for analysis. Since the land is still technically fair game, at some point the prospector needs to decide whether he's going to stake a claim on it. Such decisions are not done rashly, though, as each claim is an investment of time, money, and physical effort.

"You have to go out there and walk the ground," Carl said. He begins with the northeast corner of the claim as his starting point, and drives his first stake into the ground. From there he walks 1,500 feet to the southeast corner, another 1,500 feet to the southwest corner, 1,500 feet to the northwest corner, then back where he started, driving stakes at every corner. The result is a fifteen-acre patch of untamed earth. There's also the option of staking a block of fifty claims.

Once the claim has been staked, it's back to the territorial government office for registration. After the office has verified the measurements and officially recorded the claim, it's Carl's for a limited period of time. If he—or another company, if he sells the claim—doesn't work it within a two-year period, the claim expires.

Sitting there listening to Carl was an otherworldly experience. His life seems idyllic, almost serene. He strikes me as a man who has come to peace with who and what he is, and has made a life around that. But just as soon as I started waxing nostalgic about the lifestyle of this hale and hearty man of the world, he began to tell me about some of the near misses he's had flying in the North. It was enough to abruptly shake me out of my wistfulness.

"If you fly these things, shit happens," he said. "That's just the way it is. They're mechanical devices, just like cars. And if you're gonna fly them, you're gonna have things go wrong. You don't fly airplanes and not have near-misses."

On one occasion, Carl was flying a DHC-2 Beaver in the High Arctic near a remote fishing lodge at Bathurst Inlet. "I was on top of the clouds, about five hundred feet off the ground, when the thing packed up," he told me nonchalantly. Maybe too nonchalantly, since the phrase "packed up" means the engine seized, leaving Carl five hundred feet off the ground with no source of power.

"I came down through the cloud and beat the plane up pretty good," he said with a chuckle, "tore the legs off the thing. I had my hands full with that one!" After a long and lonely night in the bush, Carl was back at it the next day.

Another time, Carl was flying a six-seat Cessna 185 Skywagon in the dead of winter at about 3,500 feet when one of the two landing skis broke off the plane and ripped right through its door, flipping the craft upside down along the way. Everything on board flew out the windows.

"I flew it for forty miles pretty much sideways with two notches of flap on and the ski still on the check cables," he said, never showing a hint of discomfort at the memory. "I flew it sideways to keep the ski out where I could see it, so it didn't beat up the airplane anymore." He landed safely in Lac La Martre, where a pilot from Yellowknife-based Ptarmigan Airways flew him back to the city.

Carl hasn't always been alone during such adventures, for better or worse. One time he was taking off with a representative from Transport Canada and the owner of Air Dogrib aboard when one of his plane's skis fell off. For Carl—who has logged more than eighteen thousand hours flying the lonely northern skies—it was another day on the job. "I just continued around and landed on the one ski," he said. "But the boys were sure a little white!"

If this all seems like old hat to Carl, it probably is. He says the key to handling an emergency situation in a bush plane is to stay focused on the task at hand. "I never get flustered, and I've never been afraid," he said. "It happens and you're too busy trying to correct the situation to be afraid of it. So up to the point where you terminate yourself, upside down or inside out or the wing falls off, you're just too busy flying the airplane to be afraid of it. Something goes wrong, and you just have to deal with it."

Deal with it again and again, it would seem, regardless of the location. Apparently Carl's adventures have not been limited to the North. "I was taking off out of Gander in a Beaver with a load of mail, one passenger, and on wheel-skis again," he said. "We were on our way to Fogo and were just off the ground when the engine seized.

"I had to go straight ahead, because I didn't have enough speed to do anything else. And the control tower kept telling me I was on fire; I guess there was flames shooting out the back of the plane. I didn't care; I kept priming the thing trying to get it going again, but all the gas was running out the back.

"Well, I went into the trees with that one. But it didn't catch on fire and we both got out, so no big deal."

Not all of Carl's flying stories involve crash landings. Two of his favourites, in fact, involve the dearly departed. The first one sees Carl transporting a body for the first time in his life. "Well, nobody had ever told me about the gases in the body," he said. "So I'm flying along in a Beaver and the body bag started shaking and moving. And I'm thinking 'What in the name of God is going on?' I thought for a while that he wasn't dead.

"But then the aroma—oh my good God, it was unbelievable. And I thought 'Holy shit man, I don't need this.' I delivered the body back to Yellowknife, but it was pretty stinky."

The Beaver was big enough to fit a body bag, but a coffin is another story. While still living in Newfoundland, Carl was tasked with flying a casket—replete with a woman's body inside—to her hometown in Change Islands for the funeral. The side door was too small to turn the coffin, so Carl had no choice but to fly with both doors open and the coffin protruding a foot out each side of the plane.

"We tied ropes underneath the airplane to keep the coffin from sliding out," he said, "but I had to do gentle turns anyway.

"Well, the deal was to land on the ice," he says. "But the wind blew the ice offshore, and I couldn't find a safe place to land. So instead I landed on the bog behind the town. After we landed, a guy came over with a horse and carriage to pick up the coffin.

"The co-pilot and me were untying the ropes, and I had to climb over the top of the coffin. I was just going up over the coffin and I said to the guy, 'Oh man, I'm sorry I have to get on top of her like this, but I gotta get over there and untie them ropes.'

"'My son,' he says, 'you're not the first one that was on top of her!'"

To this day Carl doesn't know how the man was connected to the woman in the coffin, though he suspects it may have been her husband.

THE DAY WOUND ON, and the sweet, smoky air in Carl's cabin filled with the stories of his life in the North. It's a life, I realized, that mirrors Joe's on a certain level, as old bush pilots all seem cut from the same fabric: the cloth of independence, freedom, and living every minute of this great gift called life. Yet there is something else these men and women share: the recognition that when things go wrong in the wilderness, people need to band together to solve problems.

Sometimes, though, there isn't anyone around to help, and you have to make your own choices. Such was the situation in which Martin Hartwell and the three passengers in his bush plane found themselves on a fateful day in late November 1972. Hartwell was flying a charter in his Gateway Aviation Beechcraft 18 from Cambridge Bay to Yellowknife with a pregnant Inuit woman named Neemee Nulliayok, a fourteen-year-old Inuit boy named David Pisurayak Kootook suffering from appendicitis, and a nurse named Judy Hill.

Something went terribly wrong en route, and the plane crashed into a hillside near Hottah Lake, north of Yellowknife and east of Great Bear Lake. Judy Hill was killed on impact; Neemee Nulliayok and her unborn child died the next night. Martin Hartwell and David Kootook survived the crash; both of Hartwell's ankles were broken.

A massive search-and-rescue effort was mounted in the days to come, but no sign of the downed plane was found. The weather was brutally cold, at times dipping toward −40°. With no help on the way and the pilot barely able to walk, David rose to the occasion and kept the pair alive as long as he could. He erected a tent from the plane's engine covers, made and tended the fires that kept them warm, fished at a nearby lake, and gathered lichen for them to eat.

Miraculously, Hartwell was found alive after thirty-one days, when a passing commercial aircraft picked up a signal from his emergency radio beacon. Sadly, David was dead by then, the result of complications related to his appendicitis.

Yet the rescuers' most grisly discovery was yet to come. When they happened upon the crash site, it became evident that Hartwell had survived by eating Judy Hill's flesh. Many observers were quick to condemn the act, but it illustrates that for all the romance associated with bush flying in remote regions, things sometimes do go terribly wrong.

CARL HAS CERTAINLY had his fair share of chilling experiences. And as I so often heard during my time in Yellowknife, Joe was there to help Carl in his times of need. "Joe's a temperamental guy sometimes, but he went out of his way to get me out of the bush," Carl said.

When Carl blew an engine on his pride and joy, the yellow Cessna 180 parked in front of his cabin, he again had to improvise the landing, this time on a remote lake sixty-eight nautical miles from Yellowknife. "So I paddled the plane to shore and got on my satellite radio and had a guy come pick me up. Well, now I need an engine."

Securing an engine for the 180 was not a problem, but getting it back to the plane was a little more challenging. Enter Buffalo Joe, the secret philanthropist. "Joe shipped the engine up from Penhold, then flew it into the bush in his Norseman. Joe brought two of his people there with him, and we changed the engine right there in the bush." The job took two days.

It's this kind of attitude, an attitude born of shared recognition of just how special life's circumstances are for northern bush pilots, that fascinates me. And as I came to spend more time reacquainting myself with Yellowknife, the North, and the people who build their lives there, I gained new appreciation for what it means to live in a houseboat on a great northern lake with a plane sitting in your now-frozen front driveway. The beauty of such a life is not lost on Carl. "Even when I flew commercially—and no matter who I flew for—it was never a job."

It struck me that Carl Clouter has likely stood on a lonely patch of tundra a number of times in his life and been the first two-legged creature ever to set foot on that piece of earth. We sat with that notion for a while, the calm silence between us, two men enjoying the moment.

He drew long on his pipe and looked out the window. "You oughta hear a bear when it comes out of its den in the spring," he said softly. "The den is starting to melt, and everything is dripping on their fur. Well, they come out and they got icicles hanging all over their fur. And when they walk, everything is tinkling, like a crystal chandelier.

"You have to be in the bush to see that."

—10—

HAY RIVER

By northern standards, Hay River is a substantial place. With a population of almost four thousand residents, it is the second-biggest in the Northwest Territories, and also one of its most affluent. The town stretches alongside the muddy waters of the river that bears the same name, streets laid out in tidy rectangles.

Yet as close as Hay River may be to Alberta (it's less than one hundred kilometres north of the provincial border), the town still has that unmistakable Northern feel. Dirt roads vie for dominance with their paved counterparts. Small, unassuming houses share streetscapes with seventeen-storey buildings. And like Yellowknife to the north, the town boasts a population of Native and non-Native residents that together bring the town's cultural mosaic to life.

That mosaic was alive and well the night the Hay River Chamber of Commerce held its annual gala, a night of food, drink, and fun where members of the town's business community come together to celebrate themselves. That night, though, was a particularly important one for the McBryans. The chamber was about to unveil a commemorative five-dollar coin that could be used as currency at any Hay River business. The face on the coin? Joe McBryan's.

If Joe was touched, it certainly didn't show. He chose not to attend the event, instead leaving those responsibilities to Mikey and Sharon. So when the president of the Chamber introduced the coin and waxed poetic about the positive impact that Buffalo Airways has had on Hay River, it was Mikey who stepped up to the microphone and made the requisite thank-you speech.

Mikey regaled the crowd with stories of Joe's disinterest in appearing at such events, telling them how he'd rather visit his mom and dad down the street than have to socialize with a crowd. It struck me that Mikey is growing into his celebrity. He swears he's not a public speaker and is terrified at the idea of "performing" in front of people, but as he held the crowd in the palm of his hand and hammed it up for the *Ice Pilots* cameraman a few feet away, I found that difficult to believe. He was in his element.

As the party wrapped up, Mikey disappeared with some friends. From what I could gather, they were off to the local sports bar for a Hay River night on the town. I had a rampie morning waiting for me the next day, so I opted for an early evening, the idea of another night drinking with Mikey was too much for me to handle.

Sharon drove me home in her fancy new Ford F-150, a rig that doesn't fit her demure personality. But I didn't argue with a free ride on this −30°C (−22°F) night. We headed straight for Buffalo's staff residence, a house the company keeps there for its Hay River rampies, overnighting pilots and truckers, and anybody else doing business with the company who needs a place to crash. It was nearing midnight, and Sharon asked me if I would prefer to sleep in their guest room, since the boys in the staff residence were likely all asleep. Somehow, I couldn't see a bunch of twentysomethings calling it an early Friday night, so I kindly declined.

Truth be told, the idea of spending a night in Joe's house was more than slightly discomfiting to me, especially given the events of earlier that evening, when I'd waited in his living room as Mikey got ready for the big gala. Joe had walked in while I chatted with Sharon and two members of the *Ice Pilots* crew, and the look on his face when he saw me in his home was enough to make me shiver in my boots. Bad enough that I'd invaded his work environment; now I had to show up at his house too? Anyway, I'd been promised the "Captain's Room" at the staff house, an invitation I might never receive again. Sure enough, the lights were on when we arrived, so I bid goodnight to Sharon.

As I made my way up the stairs of the house, though, I couldn't help but reflect on Sharon, a woman who has played such an important role in the lives of all the McBryans, but manages to fly so low under the radar. In some ways, she reminds me of the women who have made their mark on the fine art of piloting in the remote northern wilderness.

Of the countless women who have flown bush planes in Canada over the past century, none resonated with me quite so much as Lorna (Bray) deBlicquy, a trail-blazing spirit who stepped out of the shadow of a stereotype and into the life of adventure she had always craved.

Born in Blyth, Ontario, on November 30, 1931, Lorna grew up in an era when it was not fashionable for women to do anything other than stay at home and raise a family. But she had other ideas. At fourteen she decided she wanted to fly, and soloed for the first time at fifteen. She took up skydiving at sixteen and became the first woman in Canada to make a parachute jump.

Lorna and her first husband, Tony Nichols, spent time in Thompson, Manitoba, and Sudbury, Ontario, where she flew bush planes and earned her instructor's licence. Her second marriage was to well-known Canadian bush pilot Dick deBlicquy, whose travels took the couple to several spots in Ontario, as well as New Zealand. Along the way, Lorna had a baby girl, but she never stopped flying and teaching. In fact, the adventure bug kept biting Lorna, and the salve she found was in moving her family to the tiny hamlet of Resolute Bay, Nunavut (then part of the Northwest Territories), on remote Cornwallis Island in the Arctic Ocean, where she flew scientists to their camps on the tundra. Needless to say, in a place populated almost exclusively by men, where darkness settles for half a year, Lorna was *very* popular.

On one occasion, Lorna was scheduled to fly into the scientific research base at Eureka. At the same time, Canada's new prime minister, Pierre Trudeau, was visiting the Arctic. Trudeau had just left Resolute Bay and was on his way to Alert. As it turned out, weather prevented Lorna from landing in Eureka, so she made her way north to Alert. Word soon got out of her impending arrival.

The prime minister landed before Lorna, and with his entourage was soon on his way down to the barracks-like room where a modest reception was to be held on his behalf. When he arrived, Trudeau noticed a cook quickly doing up the buttons on his white shirt.

"Oh, you don't have to do anything special for me," Trudeau said. "Just be yourself."

Quickly gathering himself, the cook countered, "But it's not for you, sir! Lorna deBlicquy is flight-planned here!"

ANY NOSTALGIC IDEAS I may have had about bush flying evaporated as soon as I opened the staff house door in Hay River. The scene that met my eyes was a combination of *Animal House, Porky's,* and *Top Gun.* Mikey's house may have struck me as reminiscent of a college fraternity, but it had absolutely nothing on this place. As I entered the living room, I was greeted by four guys strewn across various tattered couches and chairs in the living room, all watching in rapt attention a movie being projected onto one of the room's blank walls. Giant chip bags and booze bottles were cast willy-nilly around the scene.

But it was no movie I'd ever seen before. In fact, it wasn't a movie at all. They were watching a live Internet feed from a bar in Saskatoon. Seems a young woman who until recently tended bar in Hay River had moved there to ply her trade. They were intermittently joking, texting her, and taking swigs from their bottles.

"You guys realize you're probably the only people on Earth watching this feed, right?" I asked. Nobody seemed to care; they were having too much fun. Adopting the when-in-Rome philosophy that has allowed me to see and do things my taste otherwise argues against, I sat down and grabbed a bottle. The movie didn't hold my attention, though, and before long I was asking where the Captain's Room was.

Jules, a Buffalo rampie who had just taken a job elsewhere and was enjoying a few glorious days of freedom before moving on, showed me to the room. If I was expecting to be ushered into the lap of luxury, I was wrong. Dead wrong.

An upturned mattress was propped against one wall, and a variety of boxes and largely unidentifiable piles of clothing crowded the floor. Sure, there was a bed, end table, and lamp; it just wasn't that easy to get to them.

"Don't run one of those CSI black lights over the bed," Jules joked. "You won't like what you see." Perfect.

The bed had no sheets, just a lone blanket crumpled in a corner. The pillow's stuffing was falling out of it. So Jules led me down to a linen closet in the basement, where I grabbed a sheet that seemed like it'd do the trick.

I lay the single sheet gingerly in the middle of the double bed, rested my head on the pillow, and promised myself not to move an inch all night. As I stared at the ceiling waiting for sleep to come, I turned to check out the reading material on the end table. It had been a long, long while since I'd read *Penthouse Letters*. But when in Rome...

MY ALARM RANG at four-thirty in the morning. The cobwebs in my head reminded me that not nearly enough time had elapsed since I closed my eyes, but I was happy nonetheless to bid a fond farewell to the captain's bed.

Though I was still bleary-eyed, it was difficult to overlook Tyler Sipos as he pulled together his breakfast in the kitchen. Tall, thick with muscles, and sporting a model's good looks, Tyler is the anchor of the Hay River operation, a hard-working rampie who knows what it takes to get ahead in Buffalo Joe's world.

Pilot Lorna deBlicquy was a tireless advocate for women in aviation. Here she flies a de Havilland DHC-2 Beaver in 1967 on Ellesmere Island, then part of the Northwest Territories. She died on March 21, 2009, at the age of seventy-seven.

"Basically, Joe likes hard workers and wants hard workers around him," he told me between mouthfuls of cereal. "And that was one thing I always made sure I did: when he wanted something done, I always got it done right away while some of the other guys spent their time kissing up to his wife and daughter."

Then Tyler threw something at me I would never in a million years have expected to hear come out of his mouth. He started quoting ancient Greek philosophers.

"I think it was Aristotle who said, 'We are what we repeatedly do. Excellence, then, is not an act but a habit.' So I wanted to make hard work a habit."

Hold on now, big boy. It's not even five o'clock in the morning, I've just rolled out of the captain's bed, undoubtedly with some rare form of communicable disease stuck to my body, and you're quoting Aristotle? Really?

But Tyler, I soon realized, is not like everyone else up here. He is Buffalo's golden boy, a strong, hard-working, no-nonsense young man, with a single focus: to dedicate himself to his work. His drive has not gone unnoticed. Once Jules announced he was leaving, Tyler learned he was getting moved to Yellowknife. Though two other rampies had more seniority than he had, Tyler was leaping ahead of them, skipping flight attending and going straight to first officer.

"It's a pleasant surprise," he said, "because I guess it doesn't happen very often." In some ways, Buffalo Airways is just like any other business: If the boss likes you, you advance more quickly than those around you. And Joe likes Tyler.

A graduate of flight school in Sault Ste. Marie, Ontario, Tyler wasn't kidding when he talked about hard work. He starts at five o'clock every morning and doesn't usually call it a day until fourteen hours later, at seven in the evening. The scope of his work largely mirrors that of his compatriots to the north: prepare the DC-3 for the scheduled morning flight to Yellowknife, which includes filling it with all the cargo that is shipped up by truck from Edmonton overnight, and run courier stops all over Hay River, dropping off parcels. Once that is done, Tyler and the rest of the Hay River crew get creative. "After that we have to do whatever needs to get done," he said as the other members of the residence slowly emerged from their rooms in greasy coveralls, grunting and grumbling their way to the refrigerator before they headed outside.

"We fix pretty much everything, because it's all old and needs work." Afternoon is the time to do pick-ups for the courier service, followed by paperwork. "Then you come in and get ready for the sked to land. The plane comes in, you put it to bed, and offload whatever freight there is." By then it's seven o'clock in the evening; the start of the next work day is only ten hours away.

But there is a light at the end of the tunnel: "On Saturdays," Tyler continued, "we get half a day off. Sunday you can work on whatever you need to work on, but you have to be there when the plane comes in at night."

"So your free time never tasted so good, right?" I asked.

"You spend it recovering and resting, mostly," he said.

But when the alternative is working as a bouncer at a bar in Barrie, Ontario, fourteen-hour days in the dark and cold of Hay River, Northwest Territories, doesn't seem that bad after all, especially when you're chasing your dream.

Rookie co-pilot Andrew Weich joined us in the kitchen. Andrew had flown as Joe's co-pilot on the sked the night before, and would be doing the same on the return flight this morning. Andrew seemed reasonably well rested, a testimony to the fact that he had graduated from the ramp to the cockpit. For Andrew and the rest of the Buffalo pilots, partying when you're flying is a serious no-no. "Legally, there has to be eight hours from your last drink and flying," Andrew said. "But our company operations manual states twelve hours."

If anything, it's reassuring to know that the guys behind the controls are sober when they're flying seventy-five-year-old planes.

AFTER BREAKFAST, it was dark and cold on the runway of the Hay River airport, and we were trying to stay warm in the aging Buffalo vans while waiting for the freighter to come in. A particularly heavy load was coming up on the truck from Edmonton that morning, and it wouldn't all fit on the sked, so an extra dc-3 had been dispatched from Yellowknife to carry it all back. While we were waiting, Doug Durrant arrived in his rig.

Doug has been driving for Buffalo for a little more than nine years. Every night at seven he leaves Edmonton with a truckload of goods bound for various destinations around the North, courtesy of Buffalo Airways. He drives through the night, then spends the day sleeping in the staff residence. Doug and two other men are responsible for starting the chain of events that keeps Buffalo's courier service in business. As Doug said: "One goin' up, one goin' down, and one off. So one left here last night at about six-thirty. I passed him halfway down." Whoever comes up on Friday night gets to spend the weekend in Hay River.

But this was not some twentysomething. Doug is a grown man, and I was struggling to see how he handled life in Alpha Beta Buffalo. "That's why we've got the master bedroom," he

There's no rest for Buffalo pilots or rampies. Winter or summer, snow or sun, the planes are as much a fixture in Hay River as they are in Yellowknife. And when winter descends, the purple haze of northern twilight makes a perfect backdrop for these gloriously simple aircraft.

laughed. "It's actually quite comfortable in there. We've got a TV, VCR, PlayStation."

Despite the surroundings, Doug knows that his part-time roommates come by their frat-boy living conditions honestly. "Most of these are young kids who are living away from home for the first time."

THE DC-3 TOUCHED DOWN with the yelp of rubber and a cloud of snow smoke. The props had barely stopped spinning before the place turned into a whirlwind of activity. Pilot A.J. Decoste and co-pilot Graeme Ferguson, both looking alarmingly awake given the hour, popped open the plane's cargo doors, and the loading began in earnest. My buddy French Larry was there too, looking decidedly less fresh.

Unlike the unloading that takes place in Yellowknife—where pallets piled high with boxes are unwrapped and individual packages tossed from van to van—the loading in Hay River has a different groove. Entire pallets weighing hundreds of pounds are hoisted from the truck onto a dolly. From there the dolly needs to be heaved, pushed, and cajoled uphill from the loading doors to the front of the aircraft. It's exhausting and back-breaking work. And if I'd ever wondered how the rampies manage to stay fit while working sixty-hour-plus work weeks, the mystery was solved. Their work *is* their fitness.

The plane loaded, I started walking back to the darkened terminal to wait for Joe's arrival and take my place in the sked back to Yellowknife. As I was walking away, A.J. called after me: "Hey, Mike! Wanna ride with us?"

My first reaction was to turn him down. After all, Joe would be flying the sked this morning, and who knows, he may be in a chatty mood. But as I was walking toward the terminal, a change of heart washed over me. Why should I wait around for something that may never happen? So I turned on my heels and ran after Graeme as he disappeared into the belly of the beast.

That was a good call. Larry was kind enough to offer me his place in the jump seat, an auxiliary fold-up seat in the cockpit directly behind the pilot and co-pilot. In retrospect, Larry probably could have kept the seat, since I spent so much time *out* of it, standing and looking out at the world before me with newborn awe.

"Where are you gonna sit?" I asked as Larry rifled through a closet in front of me, pulling out various down parkas, engine tents, and engine donuts and placing them in the only patch of open floor space on the overstuffed plane.

"Don't worry about me," he said, tossing the items in a heap on the floor, curling up on it, and closing his eyes. When you work as hard as a Buffalo rampie does, you don't miss an opportunity to catch up on your sleep.

Still, I'm amazed that he could slumber through the cacophony that followed. Take-off in a DC-3 is unlike anything I've ever experienced, even though I'm a fairly seasoned traveller. The engines roared to life with a throaty growl, then burst into a mechanized frenzy as A.J. gunned the throttle. The DC-3 rumbled down the tarmac like a runaway train.

The plane was bouncing, shaking, and creaking, and for a minute I thought to myself, this may be this particular DC-3's last flight. Then, with a grace that belied her age, the "3" lifted gently off the ground. We were airborne.

The flight from Hay River to Yellowknife clocked in at around fifty minutes, but time stood still for me that morning. Until that trip, I had been strictly a sidesaddle rider in aircraft, occasionally looking outside at the landscape *beside* me. Sure, you get to see the world outside, but it's almost like looking at things in the past tense.

And even then, I don't think I'm much for looking out plane windows anymore. These days, getting on a jet is a chance to catch up on some reading or to get ahead in my work. Looking out the window to marvel at the sights, particularly the ethereal vastness of the morning sky? A thing of the past.

But to be in the DC-3's cockpit and look at the world as it unfolds in *front* of you is to be thrown upside down in time and space. This is looking at the world in the future tense, a chance to see and feel the limitless potential humankind holds in its hands. No wonder Joe rarely misses a chance to fly.

Look confusing? Though pilot Rob Zonneveld did his damnedest to teach me the finer points of aviation using Buffalo Joe's flight simulator, I never really got comfortable behind the controls of the aircraft. In other words, I crashed—a lot.

And while it's pure heaven on the other side of the metal tube, the inside of the DC-3 is all business, a dizzying array of knobs, dials, levers, and switches. To my untrained eye, there were very few electronic instruments. Maybe that's why A.J. and Graeme never took their hands off the yoke or stopped fiddling with things. Their confidence was palpable, their expertise obvious. I was in good hands.

The nose of the plane—so close I felt like I could reach out and touch it—dipped and weaved in the air, like a bobber on a lake. The noise in the cockpit was deafening, so I turned to my iPod to get my message across to my hosts.

This is so f*!king cool! I typed, holding the screen in front of A.J. He laughed, then motioned to an ancient set of light-green headphones dangling on the wall in front of me. With the headset on and microphone placed strategically in front of my mouth, communication with the boys became easier. Mostly, though, I just listened. Graeme and A.J. chatted about the rest of their days: skidooing, shopping, catching up on some much-needed rest.

I wasn't much in the mood for talking, anyway. As I stood in the cockpit behind the pilot's and co-pilot's seats, my jaw was glued shut as I watched the world wake up. As we grew ever closer to Yellowknife, the darkened sky began to brighten slowly. Below us, the vastness of Great Slave Lake eased into view, shorelines of grey and black forming a gently curving frame around a white canvas. To the right, the sun began to rise, throwing rays of orange light across the sky. For the briefest of instants, I was one with the gods.

And I saw clearly, perhaps for the first time in my life, what it really means to fly.

11

FINDING CHUCK

wasn't sure if it was safe to say that Joe was starting to like me, because in all honesty, I had no idea. I was pretty sure he'd got used to the *idea* of me and was probably okay with running into me at all hours of the day or night, weekdays or weekends. But *like* me? That was a stretch.

Either way, I wasn't immune to the ravages of Joe's mood swings, a development that, if nothing else, at least made me feel like part of the Buffalo family, albeit a transient part. On some days he seemed genuinely pleased to see me. Other times he simply tolerated me. Then there were those uncomfortable instances when he patently couldn't stand me, when he started grumbling about being a commodity, and about me sucking his brain dry solely for my own personal profit. Those occasions were becoming fewer and farther between, but they still happened. And when they did, they weren't very pleasant. One Sunday morning, he barked at me: "I could write that goddamn book better than you."

"Joe, that's like me saying I could fly a DC-3 better than you," I replied, holding my turf just a little against the boss.

He didn't give in, though I could tell I'd made my point. "I could write it better because I was there," he said, softened somewhat.

Thankfully, Joe was not immune to sharing friendlier moments with me too. And on those rare occasions when he did open up, I felt blessed for the glimpse I got into what has been a truly remarkable life. They also gave me a little more insight into what makes Joe McBryan tick. And as much of a man's man as he is, I think Joe harbours a fair bit of fear. When it comes to the book, he fears two things: that I will not tell his story accurately, and that people will not believe a word of it.

I can understand why. Some of his stories are so outlandish that most people would shake their heads. Sure, Joe embellishes his tales a bit, but as an old cowboy friend of mine used to say, "Don't ever let the truth get in the way of a good story!" Truth or not, when Joe is on a storytelling roll, he is captivating.

A couple of the *Ice Pilots* crew and I were sitting around in the Buffalo Airways kitchen one Saturday morning, and Joe was regaling us with a tale of how one of his first planes—his prized Noorduyn Norseman—was wrecked in August 1970. "If you put it on film or in a book," he said as he washed the dishes, "it would be straight bullshit. Nobody would ever believe it."

So here goes. Joe wasn't flying the Norseman at the time; one of the pilots working for him was shuttling nine aboriginal firefighters from a lakeside bush camp to various hot spots in the area. On takeoff one morning, the pilot made the mistake of switching his fuel selector to a dead tank. The engine quit shortly after that, requiring the pilot to circle back around and land on the lake. Lacking sufficient power and speed, the pilot couldn't round out the plane enough and dug the floats into the water, flipping the Norseman upside down in the lake, where she floated perfectly, cockpit submerged, the floats keeping her from sinking.

As it turns out, the aboriginals on board were not particularly strong swimmers, Joe told us. "So the pilot's stuck in the cockpit, but nobody will go help him because they can't swim. And they're all yelling 'C'mon Bob! C'mon Bob!' and firing life jackets at him." The pilot finally extricated himself from the cockpit, a bit bloodied from the impact, but otherwise unhurt.

With little other choice, the passengers decided to swim for shore, but not before shedding their clothes. "But before they do, they find one of the first aid kits floating in the water, and all decide to wrap some gauze bandage around their heads, in case they get hurt. So now they're out there naked, with only a gauze band wrapped around their heads."

Luckily, the Norseman's pilot—a gentleman by the name of Bob Gauchie—was able to convince his passengers that swimming to shore might not be the most advisable course of action, given that there was no imminent danger and the plane would float indefinitely. Instead, the ten men set to the weighty task of paddling the plane to shore. "He got them to all kneel down on the floats and start paddling the airplane toward the shore," Joe said. "There's a current in that lake, but it's the only thing you can do if you're upside down."

Meanwhile, the firefighting camp was now abuzz with activity. Among those on shore was a rookie helicopter pilot with his Bell 47 chopper, which had been equipped with floats for water landings. After witnessing the Norseman crash, the helicopter pilot jumped into action, grabbing his engineer and hopping in the chopper.

"But instead of landing beside the airplane," Joe said, "he hovers over it and looks at everything going on underneath him. Well, the guys on the floats all panic and grab the skids [the ski-like metal strips that helicopters land on] and start climbing on. Well, the helicopter flips over too, and ends up upside down in the water too!" Now everybody is swearing at everybody else—a complete mess.

For act three of this comedy of errors, enter the remaining firefighters, who were standing on shore watching both the plane and the helicopter crash into the water. With no boats at their behest, they were forced to turn to their collective ingenuity to mount a rescue effort. They strung together a series of metal fuel kegs and assembled a makeshift raft, paddling feverishly out to the crash site. "They didn't know how many people were dead or maimed or hurt," Joe said.

Apparently the firefighters were not particularly adept sailors, though, because the raft came apart halfway to their destination. The knots had untied and the ropes fallen off. "So now," Joe said almost in hysterics, "each guy is holding onto a fuel drum. They got the whole fucking camp out there in the lake floundering around and screaming and hollering and blaming each other!"

At around the same time, Joe was flying back from the High Arctic community of Cambridge Bay, listening intently to all the chatter on the radio about a Norseman and a helicopter crashing. "I thought they had crashed in mid-air," he said.

By the time Joe returned to Fort Smith to refuel, he was still no clearer on what had happened at the crash site. All he knew was that people were calling for ambulances to be readied for those arriving from the crash site. Of course, Joe thought the worst.

He was mistaken. The reason ambulances were needed, Joe said, was for their blankets, which would help warm the drenched survivors in the cool night air. Nevertheless, the scene was nothing short of unbelievable to Joe's eyes. "They all had these grey blankets wrapped around them like capes and white bandages wrapped like bandanas around their heads."

Incredibly, nobody was hurt. "When I got out there the next morning and looked at the situation, I was convinced this was a straight bullshit story, bar talk," Joe said. "And you know what? We never, ever told that story much because it was just too stupid to believe. The only people who believe that story are the forestry guys, the helicopter pilot, my crew, and the nine Indians from Fort Rez who were down on their hands and knees trying to paddle because they couldn't swim."

IF THERE'S A SHRED of truth to Joe's story, it helps show that even the best northern bush pilots find themselves in the occasional sticky situation. Call it an occupational hazard. Bob Gauchie, who was flying the Norseman when it flipped in the lake, knows that all too well. Though Gauchie's legacy as a bush pilot reaches far across the North, he is most remembered for the fifty-eight days he survived in a downed bush plane in the Arctic wilderness in February and March of 1967.

On February 2, 1967, Gauchie was making his way back to Yellowknife from Cambridge Bay, where he had dropped off a group of engineers. It was a bright, clear day, but brutally cold.

At one point, the cockpit thermometer bottomed out at −58°C (−72°F). When Gauchie was about 350 kilometres (220 miles) northeast of Yellowknife, the weather deteriorated to the point that he was forced to land his ski plane and wait it out. He set out again the next day, but he got disoriented in a whiteout and his compass failed. With no fuel left, Gauchie was forced to land on Samandre Lake, near the eastern shores of Great Bear Lake. He was about 300 kilometres (185 miles) off course. He was horrified to find that neither his radio nor his two emergency beacons were working.

Luckily, Gauchie had several sleeping bags in the plane, five days of rations for five people, and eighteen kilograms (forty pounds) of arctic char he was bringing home for his wife. With little else to do, Gauchie bundled up—and waited. The temperature sat near −60°C (−76°F) for two weeks.

Time passed slowly. The official search was called off. And still Gauchie waited.

On the twenty-fifth day of this living hell, Gauchie heard a plane pass overhead, and fired a flare. Nothing.

Over the next several weeks, more aircraft passed overhead. None noticed his plane, an indiscernible speck on the vast canvas of snow below.

Other than the wolves that kept him constant company, Gauchie passed the time cold and alone. He had eaten so much char that he could no longer stand the taste of it, but it was the only thing keeping him alive.

Finally, after Gauchie had spent fifty-eight days trapped on the lake, a plane passed overhead. Gauchie fired off two flares. The plane turned around.

When the pilots landed on the lake, Gauchie was ready for them. He was emaciated and had a long, unkempt beard, but had not lost his sense of style. He stood there as they approached, a blue suitcase in his hand. When they got out of their plane, the first thing he said to them was "Have you got room for a passenger?"

He has not eaten fish since.

JOE MUST HAVE STARTED feeling comfortable with me that morning, because shortly after telling his Norseman story, he invited me into his office. I'd been in there before—on my first day at Buffalo, when Mikey brought me in to show me Joe's

Two of Joe McBryan's greatest passions are vintage cars and vintage planes. The DC-3 in this photo—"Summer Wages," named for a song by Canadian folksinger Ian Tyson—is one of the most famous in the Buffalo fleet. It flew in the eleventh wave of the invasion of Normandy in World War II.

A bushman to the end, Chuck McAvoy poses in front of his beloved Fairchild 82. Ironically, the plane was the main competitor for the Noorduyn Norseman, a plane Buffalo Joe continues to fly to this day.

collection of aviation books ("Into the mind of chaos," he had said then as he opened the door), but I'd never had the chance to get a feel for the place as a guest of Joe's. Until now, that is.

The office is a testimony to Joe's life and passions: aviation, his family, and vintage automobiles. In fact, it's more like a museum, or perhaps an antique shop, than an office. It is dominated by an Indian Chief Centennial motorcycle sitting beside Joe's desk. A neon Route 66 sign hangs overhead.

Photographs of classic cars from the 1940s, 1950s, and 1960s—mostly Fords and Mercurys, Joe's favourites—pepper the walls, and die-cast models of planes and cars fight for space on the shelves with hundreds of aviation books and manuals of every description. A beautiful wooden propeller sits in another corner of the room, festooned with pairs of intricately embroidered moosehide mitts and slippers.

An old Streamliner toboggan—the kind with wooden slats and red metal runners—hangs from the ceiling in a corner of the room. Underneath it are cases filled with old aviation instruments, leather pilot's goggles, the yoke of a long-forgotten plane. My search revealed old magazines of collectible cars and instrument panels salvaged from the cockpits of obsolete planes. The cockpit door from an old aircraft is mounted directly onto one of the office's doors.

One of the photographs on the wall, its edges beginning to yellow with the passage of time, is of the Grade 9 class from the Federal Day School, Hay River, Northwest Territories, spring 1960: Joe's class. Picking out the Buffalo patriarch is not the easiest task, but after scanning the faces for a while I settled on a young man with a heavy pompadour, the coif Joe wears to this day. Another photograph sees a much younger Joe—perhaps eight or nine years old—feeding a magnificent sled dog.

All of it speaks to that elusive, soft side of Joe McBryan I had been so longing to find. Just when I was beginning to think that Joe might never open up to me, here I was sharing time and space with some of his most prized possessions. The door of the silver Fox Moth that was Joe's playhouse as a child is also here, the words "MCAVOY DIAMOND DRILLING AND DEVELOPMENT COMPANY, LTD. YELLOWKNIFE, NWT" still clearly visible in red block lettering.

Among all this, the thousands of bits and pieces that collectively form the backdrop of Joe McBryan's life, there is one object that says more about Joe than any other. It's a small, yellowing, canvas-covered case, whose leather corners and leather handle are drying with age. Locked to its handle is an old silver pocket watch, and attached to the pocket watch chain is a nondescript plastic sleeve. Inside that sleeve is a carefully preserved bit of fabric only 10 centimetres long by 2.5 centimetres wide (4 inches by 1 inch). The canvas is the exact same shade of green as the planes in the Buffalo fleet. "Buffalo green," they call it in Yellowknife.

Joe, it seems, was not the first one to use the colour on an aircraft. The fabric is a piece of canvas from Chuck McAvoy's Fairchild 82 bush plane, which disappeared in 1964. Joe would spend the next thirty-nine years searching for his mentor.

WHILE JOE WAS GROWING UP at the Gordon Lake Mining Camp in the 1950s, Chuck McAvoy was developing his reputation as a living legend, a fearless bush pilot who thought nothing of braving the toughest conditions the North could throw at him to shuttle prospectors, adventurers, and loners to the far-flung reaches of the Arctic. Chuck was everything young Joe wanted to be: strong, brave, independent, and very capable in the pilot's seat.

Chuck took Joe under his wing and treated him like a little brother. On slow days at Gordon Lake, Chuck threw Joe in his single-engine Cessna and taught him the care and control of an aircraft. Under Chuck's tutelage, Joe learned the fine art of bush flying: how to assess the weather, land on a frozen lake, read the subtle clues offered by the land, and find your way out to the middle of nowhere—and back home again. To Joe, Chuck was larger than life itself. So when Chuck told Joe that he was going to make a hell of a bush pilot one day, Joe took it to heart.

In Chuck, Joe found a mentor worthy of emulation. In his years of bush flying, McAvoy had developed a reputation as the bad boy of northern skies, a standing he rightly deserved. He would regularly take off and land in the dark, a practice

Fred Carmichael,
NWT's First Aboriginal Bush Pilot

BORN in 1935 and raised on a trapline near Aklavik, Northwest Territories, Fred Carmichael lived in a tent throughout his childhood and teenage years, running dogs and working as a trapper. He received his private pilot's licence in 1954; four years later he became the first aboriginal person in the Northwest Territories to get a commercial pilot's licence.

Fred started Reindeer Air Service in 1959 and flew old warplanes like the DC-3 and C-46. He built a reputation as a positive role model for aboriginals throughout the Northwest Territories and employed Native people throughout his airline. In 1982, he launched Antler Aviation, followed eight years later by Western Arctic Nature Tours, which introduced the stark beauty of the North to visitors from the world over.

Fred also served his people when not in the air. In 2000, he was elected president of the Gwich'in Tribal Council. In 2002, he was appointed chair of the Aboriginal Pipeline Group, an aboriginal group advising on the development of the proposed Mackenzie Valley Pipeline, which will carry natural gas more than 1,100 kilometres (680 miles) along the Mackenzie Valley to southern Canada.

In 2006, Fred was inducted into the Aboriginal Business Hall of Fame. The Aklavik airport is named for him.

verboten by Transport Canada. He was as renowned for his daring aerial stunts as for slugging it out in the Gold Range bar.

Chuck was much more than a rebel. He participated in almost every search-and-rescue operation mounted in the North and had an uncanny knack for bringing home lost souls well before anyone else—even the air force. In May 1960, Chuck came back with two survivors who had spent almost three weeks stranded in a remote section of the Northwest Territories' Nahanni Valley. Nobody else had been able to find them.

Given Chuck's prowess in the cockpit, you can understand Joe's shock when—on a warm spring day in 1964 with a brand new commercial pilot's licence in hand—Joe was told that Chuck's plane had disappeared. Joe had just returned to his home in Hay River, and his first job was going to be flying Chuck's Fairchild 82. "But when I got to town, they said 'Chuck's missing,'" Joe recalls.

It was June 9, 1964, the day thirty-one-year old Chuck was supposed to have taken two American geologists—Albert Kunes and Doug Torp—to a remote lake some 600 kilometres (370 miles) northeast of Yellowknife in the canvas-skinned single-engine float plane. They never arrived.

Their disappearance sparked a full-scale search for much of the next two months. In addition to a host of private pilots— all of whom were acquainted with the dynamic personality of Chuck McAvoy—the Royal Canadian Air Force (RCAF) offered search-and-rescue crews from Winnipeg, Vancouver, Nanaimo, and Cold Lake, Alberta, to aid in the hunt. In total, they flew almost 1,300 hours over some 600,000 square kilometres (231,500 square miles) of lonely Barrenlands searching for the downed plane, to no avail.

The mystery of Chuck's disappearance was deepened by the fact that search conditions were ideal throughout that entire summer. The sun shone almost twenty-four hours a day, and the skies proved clear and bright most days. Yet despite hundreds of sets of eyes and as much manpower as the air force could dedicate, there was absolutely no sign of the Fairchild or the three men. The RCAF had no choice but to conclude that either the men had died in an inflight fire, or they lay at the bottom of one of the thousands of unnamed lakes that dot the tundra. Either way, the official search was called off.

Like many other Yellowknifers, Joe refused to accept Chuck's disappearance without a fight. For months to come, pilots of all stripes donated their planes, time, and money to continue the search for the Fairchild. Each time, a disappointed pilot would return to Yellowknife with the same report: no sign of Chuck.

Others ultimately grew accustomed to the notion that they would never see Chuck or his plane again, but Joe was not so easily convinced. For the next thirty-nine years, one month, and twenty-six days, Joe made the search for Chuck his personal holy grail. He spent countless hours on solo flights across the lonely Barrenlands looking for his friend and mentor, and never failed to remind other pilots to keep their eyes peeled for Chuck.

By some cruel twist of fate, it was not Joe's lot to solve the mystery of his old friend. That distinction fell into the lap of a twenty-four-year-old helicopter pilot from rural Saskatchewan named Curtis Constable. On August 3, 2003, Constable was transporting a crew of four young geologists back to their camp near Lupin Lake, about 300 kilometres (185 miles) southeast of the Arctic Ocean community of Kugluktuk, flying a route they

Max Ward: The Entrepreneur Bush Pilot

HE was a handsome, charming young man who etched his name across the history of the northern skies like few others have.

Maxwell William Ward was born November 22, 1921, and like so many of his pioneering compatriots, gained flying experience in the military as a member of the Royal Canadian Air Force. Soon after leaving the force, Ward bought a de Havilland Fox Moth and started his first company, the Polaris Charter Company. After one of many battles with bureaucratic forces that would define his career, Max closed the company in 1951.

Two years later he was back, this time with a de Havilland Otter and a licence to operate a commercial air service. In 1953, he opened Wardair. Attracted by its relatively large payload, mining companies took to the Otter, and the airline grew rapidly. Max added many planes to his fleet, and he was responsible for ferrying thousands of tons of food, animals, and equipment to the far-flung corners of the territory.

But Max had even bigger dreams and was soon flying Canadians overseas to tropical destinations. By the mid-1970s, Wardair was Canada's largest international air charter carrier. By 1984, the airline was flying scheduled routes throughout the North and West, making a name for itself with the first-class service it offered to all its passengers.

Max sold Wardair to competing Pacific Western Airlines in 1989, which ultimately became part of Canadian Airlines.

had traversed many times before that summer. It was a well-travelled route that led to the Lupin Mine. Something caught Constable's eye sixty metres (two hundred feet) below: a glint of sun off a piece of metal on the tundra.

Constable landed the helicopter to investigate further. As he walked closer, he became the first human being in thirty-nine years to lay eyes on the Fairchild, lying serenely camouflaged atop a pile of sun-bleached rocks.

"THERE'S CHUCK'S AIRPLANE," Joe said to me as we lingered over a picture of the wreckage, a nondescript metal frame spread gently over a small patch of tundra. "Try finding that in the bush."

It wasn't long before the men realized they had stumbled upon something important. Human remains and camp equipment were strewn about the area. Constable's most important discovery was Chuck's wallet, its contents still largely intact despite the passage of time and the ravages of weather. Among the items he found inside was a membership card for the Flamingo Las Vegas. Yup, that was Chuck all right.

Joe was relieved that the mystery of Chuck's disappearance had been solved, but the irony of the discovery was not lost on him. "I still can't believe that little prick found him," he said. "I looked for him for thirty-nine years. I was looking for Chuck longer than that kid was alive." The discovery made headlines across Canada.

Before the discovery, many theories had floated around about what had happened that fateful day back in 1964: a makeshift repair job Chuck had performed earlier on a wheel caused the crash; Chuck got lost and ran out of fuel; the plane crashed through the ice.

To the contrary, Joe says the state of the plane shows that it was a controlled crash in level flight, as if it were taking off or landing. In Joe's mind, an engine failure sent the three men to their untimely demise. Still, the fact that the fuselage and wings were intact shows that Chuck flew the plane to the very end, trying to bring it down for a landing where no plane had ever landed before. In fact, other than fire damage to the engine compartment and cockpit, the rusting frame still looked very much like an airplane.

In classic McBryan style, Joe was not satisfied with merely learning the details of the crash. He needed closure, and he knew others were feeling the same way too. So Joe organized a trip to the crash site for McAvoy's siblings and the geologists' families, some of whom came from as far away as New Jersey. It was a moving experience for everybody, Joe included.

Yet not everyone was quite as touched when news of Chuck's discovery reached the outside world, particularly Jim McAvoy, who was seventy-two at the time. For Jim, Chuck's death had been a foregone conclusion. It was just a matter of time. "He was a lousy pilot," Jim said of his younger brother in a 2003 *National Post* article. "He didn't have much experience and he would try to outdo me all the time and he wasn't capable of it."

"I don't feel anything," Jim said of the discovery of his brother's plane, his lack of emotion likely the result of years of disagreement between the two about how best to run their charter airline. "He and I didn't get along too good. That was a long time ago."

Although he didn't mention them, Joe's feelings on the subject are vastly different. To this day, Joe keeps a scrapbook in his office that is dedicated solely to the search for and discovery of Chuck's Fairchild 82. The heavy binder is stuffed with newspaper and magazine clippings, photographs, original Royal Canadian Air Force search-and-rescue reports. We pored over its pages, the silence heavy between us. He pulled a photograph from a protective plastic sleeve and laid it on his desk for me to see. It was the scene he witnessed back in 2003 when he landed at the crash site for the first time.

"This is the whole scene," he said softly. His fingers traced the image and came to rest on a skeleton lying near the plane. "That's Chuck there."

It was Joe, of course, who brought Chuck—and his plane—home. This time it was on a DC-3.

12

SUMMER DAYS

Summer is the time in the North when all the promises of spring—those little teasers that begin with ever-increasing sunshine and end when the last piece of ice melts off the last lake—come true. People who have spent the past couple of months slowly becoming accustomed to the idea of warmth and light rush out of their homes in droves. Like the flowers that burst into bloom on the lands around the city, the residents of Yellowknife explode outdoors, eager to take in all that this glorious season has to offer before it fades into yet another grey winter.

People move more slowly now too. In winter, Yellowknifers hurry from place to place and task to task, hunched over and bundled up against the bite of winter. Now, the pace is decidedly more relaxed. People walk as though they've got nowhere else to be but *this* place at *this* time. Even the cars move slowly, cruising down Franklin Avenue, downtown Yellowknife's main drag, as if every day was cause enough for a Sunday drive.

In some ways, the summer version of Yellowknife—particularly Old Town—is reminiscent of a seaside village. Great Slave Lake seems more like an inland sea than a lake. The wide water is a constant backdrop; boats come and go from docks peppered along the shorelines; houseboats bob gently in the sheltered waters of Back Bay; float planes roar to life with a splash. There are even fishermen hawking the day's catch from the backs of their pickup trucks.

Away from the water, colour has returned to the landscape. The white and grey of winter and spring have given way to glorious green. Most people walk around in shorts, although I am always surprised at the number of people who opt for jeans and jackets, even when the temperature pushes into the twenties (seventies Fahrenheit). Maybe on some level they don't trust the sun, having been deceived by it one too many times.

Life at Buffalo Airways takes on a decidedly different groove in summer too. Though there is still a buzz of activity in the hangar—nobody whose last name is McBryan ever really goes on holiday—the place seems more relaxed, friendlier. People smile more, bark less, and seem to have more time to enjoy themselves. Maybe that's why the Omni TV crew chooses this time of year to pack up its gear for a few months before returning in September: happy, contented people do not make for intriguing television programming.

"It's better TV in the winter," Mikey said one sunny afternoon. "Plus summer is boring, because it's actually nice. Everyone loves coming to work; it's like summer camp."

The nature of business at Buffalo Airways changes too. Sure, Mikey and friends are still running charters to all corners of the Northwest Territories and Nunavut, but the jobs are fewer and farther between. The Mackenzie Valley run, one of the cornerstones of Buffalo's winter business, grinds to a halt, as barges use the Mackenzie River to carry hundreds of thousands of pounds of food and other goods to the communities of Déline, Tulita, Norman Wells, and Fort Good Hope.

Planes that have stood long dormant jump to life. The change is particularly acute for the CL-215 water bombers, which are enlisted into firefighting service by various provincial and territorial governments as soon as the snow is off the ground. Every pilot capable of flying one of those strange, amphibious aircraft is scrambled to wherever the whims of nature take him. I traded text messages with Scott Blue as he headed down to Fort McMurray, Alberta; Justin Simle was in Fort Simpson.

In fact, firefighting is a huge part of Buffalo Airways' business, accounting for approximately half of its entire annual revenue. I suspect there are a couple of reasons why this critical element of the Buffalo puzzle fails to make it to the television screen with any regularity. First of all, the television crew is simply not around during much of the firefighting season. Perhaps more importantly, Buffalo's firefighting contracts are all with provincial or territorial governments, which are not particularly keen on having the things they pay for immortalized on video, presumably for insurance and liability reasons.

It's too bad, really, since from what I can tell, firefighting is some of the most exciting flying a pilot can do, period. There is nothing commonplace about flying a DC-3, DC-4, or C-46, but for adrenaline junkies, fighting fires is the way to go.

Cameraman Sean Cable has had more than his fair share of experiences during his years on the *Ice Pilots NWT* crew. Here he gets uncomfortably close to a northern fire under attack by Buffalo's CL-215 water bombers.

Rick Sinotte is one of those guys. Small, spry, and boasting a weathered face that you can't help but like, Rick is a gun for hire, a pilot who works for Buffalo on a contract-by-contract basis as the situation dictates. Rick flies one of Buffalo's two Beechcraft Barons, which serve a very important role during firefighting operations. They're the "bird dogs."

In the world of aerial firefighting, the bird dog is the spotter, the plane that safely leads water bombers into and out of the action over a fire. Though a variety of aircraft are used as bird dogs around the world, their task is primarily the same. "In conjunction with the air-attack officer, we do the reconnaissance over the fire and assess what resources are needed there to contain that fire," he told me one warm summer afternoon in the Pilots' Lounge.

The air-attack officer then directs the land and air firefighting operation. "We call in the water bombers, then show them what we want them to do and where we want them to drop," Rick said. "The air-attack officer watches the drop to make sure it goes where we wanted it to go."

Rick has been flying for forty-five years, but he still gets excited when talking about the thrill of flying a small plane through clouds of smoke some twenty metres (sixty-five feet) above the burning treetops. "It's fun flying," he said with a wry smile. Yet despite the apparent risk of his work, Rick is quick to set the record straight. "It's like anything else," he told me. "There's a real safe way to do it. And that's what we do."

FIREFIGHTING IS OLD HAT for a guy like Rick. Over the five decades he's been a bush pilot, he's seen and done just about everything there is to see and do behind the controls of a plane. Then there's Scotty Blue, who sits squarely on the other side of the spectrum. Sure, Scotty has been flying for several years now, but the summer of 2011 is his first in the right seat of the CL-215 water bomber (luckily, he fits!), a position that completely changes his view on life at Buffalo Airways.

"Honestly, I was wondering what my future at Buffalo would be like," a hungover Scott confided in me one afternoon as we chowed on a delicious Sunday brunch at Thornton's Wine & Tapas Room (located right beside the Yellowknife Shooting Club). "But you fly the Duck [CL-215] for a day and you're like, 'Holy crap, I may have been thinking about beelining to the airlines, but I don't have to do that anymore. I might be quite content doing this.' Honestly, I don't think there's too much flying out there that is more fun than water bombing. It's the most exciting type of flying I've ever done. It's a big reason why

I've worked at Buffalo as long as I have: I always wanted to get into the water bombers."

To hear Scotty tell it, to see the gleam in his eyes, his long arms gesticulating wildly, his voice getting louder with each sentence, is to realize that water bombing is testosterone flying at its best. "You're on standby, so you're sitting around the tanker base doing nothing all day long. Then the alarm goes off and you run out to the plane—you don't even know where you're going. You start the plane and let the oil warm up, and that's when they give you the coordinates of your destination."

Once in the air, Scotty and his pilot—in conjunction with the bird dog and the air-attack officer—find the closest suitable lake and make the first of what can be dozens of round trips between the fire and the lake in a single day. And when the lake is just a few minutes from the fire, the plane can drop fifteen to twenty loads of water every hour. "It can be repetitive like anything, but the rush of it is hard to describe. You look ahead and there's a whole bunch of planes around, and there's fire and smoke everywhere."

"Sounds scary," I said.

"There was a moment earlier this summer where we were flying through some smoke over Slave Lake and it got really dark and I was a little scared. I've heard stories of embers coming in through the ventilation system and stuff like that. So you've gotta be on your toes."

Indeed. Water bombing is among the most technically challenging flying there is. The plane scoops up about 5,445 kilograms (12,000 pounds) of water in seconds, and dumps it even more quickly. With such significant weight changes occurring every few minutes, pilots have to be aware of what's happening around them at all times, and ready to adapt at a second's notice.

One of the most demanding moments comes when the plane skims the water with its probes extended (the probes allow the water to enter the plane's belly tanks). The resistance at that moment is so great that some have equated it with hitting a brick wall. "You have to go to total take-off power as soon as you hit the water," Scott said. "Ten seconds later you pull the probes up, the plane starts accelerating, and you take off."

For Scotty Blue, to step into the cockpit of "the Duck" (a CL-215 water bomber) was a reaffirmation of why he joined Buffalo in the first place. Few airlines can offer young pilots such an eclectic array of aircraft and missions.

Yellowknife Light and Dark

AT a latitude of 61°28' N, Yellowknife is 512 kilometres (318 miles) south of the Arctic Circle. That may seem like a fair distance, but it still means the city experiences huge fluctuations in the amount of light it receives throughout the year.

In the dead of winter, Yellowknifers get about five hours of daylight, between 9:00 AM and 2:00 PM. Then the days get longer and longer. By late April, the sun rises before 4:00 AM and doesn't set until 8:00 PM. On June 21, the longest day of the year, the sun shines all day except between 10:00 PM and 2:00 AM, and even then it's still light out, though the sky takes on a quiet, dusky hue.

The same thing happens in reverse when the water is dumped. "As soon as you drop, the plane instantaneously wants to climb, because you've just dropped twelve thousand pounds of water," he said.

Ultimately, while water bombing may be the adrenaline rush a guy like Scott needs to stay happy and engaged, it's not the most predictable employment. Water bomber pilots operate at the whim of Mother Nature. If the fires burn, you fly. If not, you sit. And as the summer of 2011 began to wane, Scott had seen only thirty-two hours in the cockpit of the Duck. It would keep him sufficiently interested and engaged to stay in the Buffalo fold—for the time being. Still, as we sat there pondering Scott's place in the aviation world, I couldn't help but wonder if his days in Yellowknife were numbered.

THE GENERAL EASE of warm temperatures and long days does not mean the essence of Buffalo will change anytime soon. As long as Joe McBryan is steering the proverbial ship, there will always be more work to do. Mikey related to me a conversation he has with Joe about this time every year:

Mikey: "I want to go on vacation this month."

Joe: "Don't take it this month. This may be the month where we get Electra work."

Mikey: "Okay, well, how about March?"

Joe: "March? Well, you never know, we always do fuel hauls in March."

Mikey: "Okay, I want to take it in June."

Joe: "June? No way, that's firefighting season."

Mikey: "Okay, what about September?"

Joe: "Well, you can't then, because that's after fire season and everyone else is on vacation."

"Every month is the wrong month." Mikey griped to me. "It's always two or three more months down the road."

Mikey says there's no seasonal rhyme or reason to life at Buffalo. "It's not really by month or season," he says. "You can have a really slow week followed by the craziest, busiest week you've ever imagined."

This lack of predictability seems to have been a huge factor in shaping Mikey's personality. He is as dedicated a worker as anyone I have ever met, but he seems to have no plans for the future, for either himself or the business. Mikey is living in the moment in every respect, and will deal with change if and when it's thrown at him. The result is a sense of liberation few people ever know.

"None of this is planned," he said as we relaxed over a cold one on his deck overlooking Back Bay. "If you drive from New York to L.A., you don't plan every rest stop along the way. It's the journey, right? And you can never guess what's around the next corner."

I find Mikey's take on things refreshing, albeit a bit uncomfortable when he starts talking matter-of-factly about the end of Buffalo Airways. Like so many people, I have come to love this quirky, renegade airline. We want it to exist, because we need to know that there is more to this world than the homogeneous, fast food, cookie-cutter crap most of us choose to ensconce ourselves in. Mikey is not bound by the same shackles.

"Look at Joe," he continued. "He went to bed one night and he was one of a hundred people flying these old airplanes. And the next day he woke up and he's the last one. And he'll either die or retire. But he can't really give up the world that he created. And it can't exist without him. Shit, we can barely exist with him sometimes."

Mikey seems to embrace his role in the scheme of things here. If Joe is the Ghost of Christmas Past and Rod the Ghost of Christmas Present, then Mikey is definitely the Ghost of Christmas Future. "For me, Buffalo Airways is the here and now. I don't care about the stories of twenty years ago about some guy who's dead now; it's already happened. I want to know what's going to happen next. I don't want to read the history books; I'm looking at Google News because I want to see what's happening now. Even newspapers are too old for me."

Just as all the McBryans perform a different job for the company, this focus on different parts of Buffalo's history— past, present, and future—seems to work. Joe is a link to the past, a bygone era whose old-school traits of hard work and "get 'er done" have kept Buffalo viable in a competitive industry with equipment that most people wrote off decades ago. Rod keeps things going on a daily basis. Without his expertise, the planes don't fly *now*, and the whole thing comes crashing down,

Buffalo Airways Virtual

IS there no end to how hard-core aviation buffs can be? Enter Buffalo Airways Virtual (www.buffaloairwaysvirtual.com), a website that allows Buffalo wannabes to fly almost every airplane in the fleet. Using software like Microsoft's Flight Simulator X—which incorporates geographical data from almost every corner of the globe (including Canada's North)—the website allows its members to replicate the company's missions or design their own.

The virtual airline started when Buffalo Airways fans Thomas Emms and Randy Kearnes presented Mikey with a prototype website. Mikey admired what Thomas and Randy were doing—and how seriously they take their online responsibilities. "These guys are physically flying more than my pilots! One guy was flying fourteen hours a day—and he was an American! If you don't fly within the first five days of signing up, you're deleted. If you don't fly within a fourteen-day period, you're deleted.

"These guys know more and care more about our planes than most people," Mikey continued, "but a lot of them can't afford to fly or never got a chance to. There are a thousand reasons why they couldn't fly, and now they can fly. So we try to support them as much as possible."

According to vaCentral (www.vacentral.net), a website that ranks virtual airlines based on an elaborate scoring system, Buffalo Airways Virtual currently ranks fifth-highest in the world, from a total pool of 192.

perhaps literally. Mikey is the visionary. For him, Buffalo is about so much more than the airplanes. It's about opportunity, and it's about seeing the world through a different lens.

"My dad and my brother just don't get it. My dad says why waste your time talking to a writer and making a book when you can be outside shovelling the walkway. But I say why waste my time shovelling the walkway when I can be talking to a writer and making a book?

"My brother says, 'Why bother?' I say, 'Why not?' "

You can't argue with the guy's success. He's one of the stars of a successful TV program. His apparel business is growing at a dizzying rate. He's got a book being written about him and his company; a website—Buffalo Airways Virtual—dedicated exclusively to fans around the world who want to simulate Buffalo flights; and even a few copycat shows "inspired" by Buffalo (*Arctic Air, Flying Wild Alaska,* and *Dust Up*). So when Mikey talks about an animated series à la *Thomas the Tank Engine,* featuring Buffalo's planes, I respect the idea's potential.

To Mikey, Buffalo's potential client base is limited, which is why looking outside the company's traditional revenue streams makes sense. "There are about fifty people in Canada who would be willing to pay sixty thousand dollars to charter one of our airplanes," he told me, adding that the TV show has probably increased their business by about 10 percent. "But on a good week, we'll get a million people watching *Ice Pilots.*

"We're no longer an airline; we're a brand."

A BIG PART of that brand is Mikey's Buffalo Airwear store, which has seen its sales grow exponentially since *Ice Pilots* came on the air. "I went from selling T-shirts on a rack behind my desk in my office to what we have now," Mikey said. And what they have now is quite something. The Buffalo Airwear store is a dedicated space in the Buffalo terminal, conveniently located for DC-3 passengers and curious passersby alike. On my first trip to Yellowknife, the store was manned by only one person, manager Peter Magill. On a return trip a few weeks later, I was surprised to find that Peter had hired a full-time assistant whose sole responsibility was to fill Internet orders.

And while those Buffalo commodities are red-hot now, things were a little tighter back in the early days of what Joe calls "Mikey's T-shirt business." "Back then, I really only sold to Europeans and the staff," Mikey told me as we took stock of the hoodies, T-shirts and even underwear filling the shelves of the little shop. "I had to be diligent because profit margins were so thin—no freebies, no deals. I even bought my own: I have never, ever taken a T-shirt for free. The same goes for my father and my brother."

Things have certainly changed. Not that Mikey is throwing product at people (I was secretly hoping he'd toss me a goodwill hoodie or some other kind of swag; it never happened), but he could if he wanted. He tells me that he is now the second-biggest buyer from North Vancouver supplier and printer Bold Merchandise, behind only Canadian rock band Billy Talent.

Yet the store represents much more than a profit centre for Mikey. Here is where he can be truly autonomous, where he can reach his creative and business potential. It's an atmosphere quite unlike that inside the hangar. "My father micromanages everything else. It's so bad that he has to sign every single purchase order. If you want to buy a can of WD-40, he has to approve it first."

JOE MAY BE CONTROLLING when it comes to the airline side of things, but you can't argue with his success. Buffalo owns almost every single plane in its fleet, something few other airlines can boast. Mikey was reluctant to get into specifics about dollars and cents with me, but I could tell he struggles with the "multi-millionaire" tag that the show has bestowed upon Joe and the rest of the McBryan clan. "It's still very expensive for the products that make the planes run: the hangar, the heat, the people," Mikey told me one night as we took in his evening dose of reality TV—this time it was *Pawn Stars,* an American show that chronicles the trials and triumphs of daily activities at Las Vegas's Gold & Silver Pawn Shop.

"Aviation is a very thin homeostasis, meaning all the money you make has to go back into the company to make more money. You only make money when you're broke and you steal from yourself before the sheriff gets it or you sell out."

That grim reality is one of the primary drivers of Mikey's endless attempts to diversify the Buffalo brand. Yet diversification comes at a cost, and Mikey knows it. It wasn't long before our conversation turned to the fact that as much as Mikey has done for Buffalo's bottom line, he is also losing his connection to its core business: flying stuff (and people) around the North.

He revealed this to me one afternoon in his office. "Look, I'm sitting here with you, and I'm not out there looking at the planes. In some respects it's like selling out." And while most of us may cringe at the notion of *selling out,* Mikey sees it as a necessary step in the evolutionary chain of any business that wants to grow.

"Say you had your favourite kind of pop from your hometown," he says, "Canmore Cola. You knew the owner, and you'd go get your can of pop, and feel good about it. Then you tell all your friends and they tell all their friends and it gets more and more popular.

"Only now, his supply doesn't meet the demand, and he has to get a bigger store. He keeps growing because the demand is there. Eventually, he'll be forced to go national, and in doing so, he turns his back on the person who got him there in the first place: you. People think that's selling out, but you're virtually forced to do it."

And if that is the route Buffalo eventually follows, so be it. Mikey will have no regrets. "The more I go down the rabbit hole of opportunity, the more I'm losing what is at our core: Buffalo Airways. Because sending a DC-3 T-shirt to Paris has nothing to do with the DC-3 flying to Hay River."

That is where the Buffalo symbiosis kicks in again, though. Mikey may be the one pushing the company to places it has never been before, but Joe, Rod, Kathy, and Sharon are the ones keeping the planes flying to the places that they've always been. The core business, it seems, is in good hands.

"Joe's the one keeping it real," Mikey said one Saturday afternoon as we watched the DC-3—with Joe at the helm—rumble down the Yellowknife runway on its way back to Hay River. "The more he tells you to fuck off, the more Buffalo is staying legit. Because once that plane stops flying, everything else comes to a grinding halt. Our heart will stop beating."

This reality has not stopped Mikey from being Mikey, though, and revelling in all *Ice Pilots* has done for him. In short, Mikey *loves* being a celebrity.

For a kid from a small town in the Northwest Territories, being thrust into the public eye can be intoxicating. I can see it in Mikey's eyes when we talk about the concept of Mikey As Celebrity. "For me," he says, "the TV show opens up the world. Before *Ice Pilots,* I was stuck seven days a week in the hanger. Now I can go on Global TV news, on *Canada AM* in Toronto. I get to meet authors, people I would otherwise never have met."

It's not like Mikey hides the fact that he loves the attention *Ice Pilots* has granted him. He calls himself "shameless" when it comes to publicity. Nevertheless, Mikey never puts on a false front for the camera or his fans. He is who he is.

"I find that most people are scared of criticism," he tells me one morning as we drive to the hangar in the glory of twenty-four-hour sunshine. "They run their lives based on what they think other people will think of them. It really holds people back."

Not Mikey. Both on and off the screen, he wins his way into your heart by marching to the beat of his own drummer. On one of the most well-loved episodes in Season Two, Mikey and Joe venture to England to inspect a few Electras that a British airline is trying to sell. Joe spends his time elbow-deep in the operations of the craft; Mikey provides comic relief. At one point, Mikey heads down to the local pub with a bunch of employees from the airline, his face completely painted in support of England's soccer team, which was playing in the World Cup that evening.

Later, fall-down drunk—he earns his stripes by guzzling a yard of ale (about 4.5 pints) without coming up for air—the youngest McBryan has forged a relationship with the seller that Joe could never manage. In some ways, that episode speaks again to the symbiosis between father and son: Joe makes sure the planes are fit enough to join the Buffalo fleet; Mikey cements ties to the client with the mortar of hops and barley.

Mikey McBryan's 10 Favourite Foods

1 Chicken wings

2 Lobster

3 King crab

4 Kraft dinner

5 Ribs

6 Big Macs

7 Hot dogs

8 Blackened steak

9 Beans and toast

10 Beer

AS IT DID in England, Mikey's celebrity status often comes in handy on the work front. There are times, however, when being one of the focal points of a hit TV show pays social dividends as well: over the course of *Ice Pilots*, Mikey has made loads of friends, both the Facebook kind and the real kind. Of these, perhaps none mean more to Mikey than Bobby Hanson and Serge Pharand, two very successful Ottawa entrepreneurs Mikey befriended at the EAA AirVenture air show in Oshkosh, Wisconsin, a few years back.

When November 27, 2010—Mikey's twenty-eighth birthday—rolled around and Mikey found himself with no plans for the big day, he called Bobby and Serge. Within minutes, the plans were set: he and his best friend Austin were on their way to Ottawa. Other than for university, it was the first time Mikey had been out of the north without doing something related to aviation.

"We land in Ottawa, and Serge shows up driving a fully decaled Buffalo Airways Chevy HHR," Mikey told me, an ever-widening grin on his face. "They take us out for this big, fancy meal and people are recognizing me left and right. It was crazy."

The visit also took Mikey and Austin to Ottawa-area air and space museums, where they were treated like royalty. "They were basically throwing the keys at me, said I could be in whatever plane I wanted to be in." Mikey took advantage of the offer on several occasions, though the highlight was his chance to sit in a plane he's admired since he was a boy: the Curtiss p-40 Warhawk, a single-seat fighter plane used extensively during World War II.

"Then they took us to an Ottawa Senators game," Mikey continues. "We had rinkside seats: leather seats, the whole nine yards. Afterwards we got to meet Mike Fisher; I got my jersey signed by him after the game."

As if this wasn't enough for someone as hockey-crazed as Mikey, the trip was only going to get better. For if there's one thing that Mikey McBryan likes as much as hockey—perhaps even better—it's establishments that combine beer with scantily clad women. "Serge and Bobby dropped us off in Hull, Quebec, at the most magnificent strip club I've ever seen!"

The next morning it was off to Serge and Bobby's private hangar, where Mikey found an astonishing array of aircraft "They open the doors and say, 'Whatever you want . . . it's yours to fly,' " he said, still only half-believing the event really happened.

"I had always wanted to fly in a fighter jet, and they had two Russian l-39 MiG training jets. While we waited for the pilot to show up, we went in a Pitts Special [a two-seat open-cockpit plane designed for aerobatics]. Now I'm completely fucking hungover from the strip club the night before, and here I am in the back of this plane doing full loops and cart rolls." The going didn't get any easier for Mikey when he eventually got in the cockpit of the fighter jet and found himself again doing loops, only this time at speeds in excess of 563 kilometres (350 miles) per hour.

Yet as much as he enjoys experiences born of his celebrity, Mikey still struggles to understand why people are so fascinated with him and his little world. In fact, it seems Mikey and his fellow stars can't go anywhere outside of Yellowknife without being recognized. In one instance, Mikey and a friend were in Vancouver, where they decided to take in Conan O'Brien's *Legally Prohibited* show. When the pair started walking up the aisle from their second-row seats to get more beer, Mikey was floored when audience members started screaming his name. "Here I am, star-struck because I'm seeing Conan O'Brien," he said, "and people are stopping *me* for pictures! That's when I really realized things had changed."

On that same trip, Mikey and his friend were sharing a few beers on the patio of a local pub, when Mikey's iPhone alerted him of an incoming message. "I have Google alerts set to search the Internet for my name," he said. Turned out a woman at the next table was Twittering to all the world that Mikey McBryan was having a beer right beside her.

Mikey's insight into the evolution of celebrity may be the one thing that keeps him from losing control. For as much as he loves it, he also knows that there is a dark side—a real dark side—to fame. "As hard as it is, you can't allow yourself to be changed by fame," he said one night as we stumbled home after yet another session at Surly's. "Otherwise it starts to wear at you, and you get to the point where you're at a restaurant screaming at the waiter because he doesn't recognize you. It's very insidious to who you are. You can see how people get caught up in it."

It certainly helps that Mikey and crew are in Yellowknife, perhaps one of the most down-to-earth places on the planet. "You get the odd snide remark," Mikey said, "but luckily I hang out with a bunch of tough rampies who can take care of people who make snide remarks."

But for the time being, Mikey is happy to roll with the benefits of stardom, whether it be flying in a Russian fighter jet or having women pay more attention to him—*way* more attention—than they otherwise would. And the show has even made it easier for Mikey to handle the daily grind of life at Buffalo Airways.

Situations that used to upset him are now seen in a whole new light. "When you're not used to seeing it on a sixty-two-inch HD television, you sometimes think that things are not going to work out and there's going to be a real disaster," he said. "*Ice Pilots* has shown me that things do work out, and there are triumphs."

Mikey's not the only one to realize this particular benefit. "Since the TV show has started, it's been a real morale booster. We don't go through as many people as we used to. Why? Because they see merit in their work. The show is now the mother. So it's no longer necessary for Joe to come up to you and say 'You did a good job.' You can just go watch *Ice Pilots*."

MIKEY IS CERTAINLY not the only member of the Buffalo crew who has felt the effects of stardom. Justin and Scott are both very popular with the ladies. Nevertheless, nobody, it seems, has let that fact go to his head. For the time being, heads at Buffalo remain level.

Even Justin, who is portrayed on the show as being as cool as they come, blushes his embarrassment when forced to talk about his new-found celebrity. Maybe it's because he's used to the attention. We take our customary seats at the Gold Range Diner, and the playful flirting between him and one of the waitresses begins almost immediately.

"Are you gonna get married yet?" she asks him, setting two glasses of water in front of us.

"I'm waiting for you!" he calls back as she makes her way to the kitchen.

"That's what you say to all the girls, Justin."

"Nope, just you, love."

This is where Justin is most comfortable, in his everyday haunts, surrounded by people he knows and feels connected to. Perhaps that is why he has stayed at Buffalo longer than any other pilot currently on the Yellowknife roster. It also goes a long way toward explaining why he feels the need to spread credit for the show's success as widely as he can, despite the fact that he's one of its biggest stars.

"I was walking through the Edmonton airport with my daughter and heard a stampede coming behind me," he says between forkfuls of the chicken cordon bleu special of the day. "I turned around and there was half a dozen girls there screaming and giggling: 'Oh my God, it's Justin Simle from *Ice Pilots!*' They picked up my daughter and started passing her around like she was a toy. It was cool, but weird at the same time." Ultimately, a very private person like Justin will look back on the *Ice Pilots* experience and appreciate it for what it was, but know that it didn't really change his world.

"It's a really neat thing that we've done here, a once-in-a-life-time opportunity," he tells me one night. "I'm grateful for the experience, but when it all goes away, I'll just keep doing what I'm doing. You can't change for anyone but yourself."

I'M NOT SURE if the same can be said for Scott, who shares heartthrob status with Justin in the Buffalo hangar. Witty, handsome, warm, and engaging, Scotty Too Tall (as he is affectionately known) has won over fans around the world with his honest and forthright take on life in the North. Scotty shares Justin's humility—he too struggles to understand why people find him so interesting—but there's no denying he loves the attention. For Scotty, being a part of Buffalo and *Ice Pilots* is the best thing that could have happened to him.

"There's lots of different perks and unique situations that we find ourselves in because of the show," he says. "You know what? It's cool to be recognized all over the place, and it's flattering when good-looking girls just want to hook up with you without really knowing anything about you."

For Scott, though, *Ice Pilots* has opened doors to experiences that go far beyond interludes with members of the opposite sex. On one particularly warm spring day, he and I were celebrating the fact that he'd just been checked out on the CL-215, opening the door to his first-ever summer of fighting fires with the water bomber. Not long afterwards, Scotty was rubbing elbows with some of Canada's biggest political figures... all because of *Ice Pilots*.

Driving home one evening, Scott came across a rally and photo shoot for the Conservative Party of Canada in support of a federal election campaign. Interested, he stopped to poke his head in, and was almost immediately recognized by security personnel, who let Scott enter the rally, even though he was not on the guest list. It didn't take long for Scott to offer Canada's most powerful political figure a tour of the Buffalo hangar; minutes later—and much to his surprise—Scott was showing Prime Minister Stephen Harper and wife Laureen through the hangar.

"That was pretty damn cool!"

But as much as *Ice Pilots* may feed the ego, Scotty believes the show helps clear up some fairly pervasive misconceptions about the life of a pilot. "A lot of people think that you go to flight school, and the next thing you know you're flying a jumbo jet around the world and drinking champagne with hot stewardesses and staying in amazing hotels," he says with an ironic chuckle. "Back in the day it may have been like that, but it's not any more. Before *Ice Pilots,* I don't think people realized how hard we work. But I think the show really gets that point across. It's a labour of love."

Labour of love, indeed. For every unique opportunity that Buffalo hands its employees, there's a thankless one waiting around the corner. Scotty knows. "You'll get a day when you have to come in early to get the plane ready, and it's –35° and the wind is howling," he describes. "So it's already hard enough to get to work as it is. Then you get there and the engines are frozen up because the heaters have unplugged overnight.

"So you get a frost fighter [a small, portable heater] to warm them up, but the frost fighter is out of gas because nobody could be bothered to fill it the night before. Then you get the fuel truck but the fuel truck doesn't have enough gas in it, so you have to go fill it up. But when you come back, you realize that it's so cold out that the fuel truck won't pump because it's frozen. So you go back inside where the freight is waiting, and the floor is slippery and it's a bitch to load. By that time, the captain has shown up and he's pissed off and yelling. Those are the real clusterfuck mornings that make you question why you're here."

IN THE MEANTIME, *Ice Pilots* is alive and well, and everyone involved with the show seems optimistic about its future.

Whether it ultimately proves as successful as other hyper-popular programs like *Deadliest Catch* and *Ice Road Truckers* remains to be seen. In the meantime, Mikey is not losing any sleep worrying about the future; he's too damn busy in the present.

Late one evening, Mikey and I were the only two left in the hangar. For a moment, the massive building was silent but for the echo of our footsteps. I was waxing nostalgic again, hoping beyond hope that there is a way to keep something as raw, as true, and as authentic as Buffalo Airways alive. And I knew that the one hope for doing that was walking right beside me.

"Do you feel a desire to keep all of this going?" I asked.

As always, Mikey surprised me with his response. I was hoping for a moment of tenderness, a whispered "Yeah" that would bond us. No chance.

"Every single company that has ever existed—and ever will exist—will fail one day, will cease to exist."

"You have a very pragmatic view of it."

"I was born in the Microsoft age," he replied, "where Microsoft was bigger than life itself, and everyone thought Microsoft would be running the world. But look around: Apple is gaining ground, things are changing, and Microsoft isn't king of the world anymore.

"General Motors was king shit for fifty years," he continued. "Hell, they built the planes that bombed Japan. And now they're getting their asses kicked by Japanese companies.

"Every company fails, especially airlines. It will eventually happen. We just have to do the best we can while we do it ... no regrets."

So much for nostalgia. That doesn't mean Mikey won't be sad when Buffalo eventually does close its doors, because I know he will. He's said as much. But for someone who's always looking down the "rabbit hole of opportunity," the death of one thing means the birth of another.

"There's a freedom in mortality," he said. "Once you realize you're gonna die, you can truly be free."

Clearly, Mikey is not stuck on the future. He is comfortable with his place in the universe. "I feel very fortunate that I understand where I'm at, because most people don't. They're lost; they don't know where they fit in; they don't know what they want to do. I know what I want to do. I want to be at work at seven-thirty tomorrow morning, make sure the planes get where they need to be, and work at any challenges that come my way during the day. I can't predict what it's gonna be, but I can predict that I'm gonna try my best."

We turned off the lights and headed toward the small green door that had marked my entry to the world of Buffalo so many months before. "Is there anything you're scared of?" I asked.

He replied without hesitation: "The one constant fear is the old man."

"Why?"

"Because in Joe's eyes, you gotta be perfect—unless you're a fuck-up, and then you're a fuck-up. And he knows I'm not a fuck-up, so I gotta be perfect."

"Why does he have such high expectations of you?

"Because he knows I can do it."

13

DEPARTURES

By August, I had spent sufficient time in the hangar, on the ramp, and in the offices of Buffalo Airways to have become, by all measures, a familiar face. For the most part, the people I crossed paths with knew who I was, what I was doing, and seemed genuinely happy to let me be a part of their lives. Well, almost everybody.

No matter what I said, Rod McBryan never really seemed to trust me. On some level, I understand. From what I hear, Rod is tired of the regularity with which engine problems and breakdowns appear on *Ice Pilots*. Sure, they make for tantalizing television, but they are rare occurrences. Yet the show makes it seem like they happen all the time. Rod takes that kind of thing personally. As a result, there's something in him that just couldn't trust me either. I guess he thought that was my modus operandi too.

And then, of course, there was Joe. For months he and I had been playing a cat-and-mouse game of epic proportions. He'd see me, then dart around a corner before I had the chance to even wish him a good morning. Other times he'd eye me with a stare so icy it would freeze the engine of a DC-3 in mid-flight. That's when *I* would turn the corner as quickly as possible.

It wouldn't have been so bad if that was how Joe always acted around me. But he'd lured me in by showing me his softer side on a couple of occasions, and I was hooked. There was that one morning in the kitchen when he told the story of growing up in Edmonton, and I'll never forget the time he let me in his office and showed me his Chuck McAvoy scrapbook. So I knew there was something there, that undercurrent of kindness and vulnerability that everybody talks about. It pulled me along, like a carrot leading a rabbit.

And so the world's longest fencing match continued.

MY DOGGED PURSUIT of Joe continued through Yellowknife's all-too-brief summer, as August began to make its uncompromising march toward autumn. Mikey and I were driving down Old Airport Road one late summer afternoon when he noticed a yellowing leaf on a nearby tree, a sight that sent him into a tailspin of emotion. Like most Yellowknifers, Mikey is not particularly thrilled by the idea of summer coming to an end, though he knows it will—and quickly.

I couldn't help but share Mikey's feelings, though for different reasons. For me, the turning of the leaves meant my time at Buffalo had nearly come to a close, another northern chapter in my life nearly written. Yet still Joe eluded me. That one magic moment, the instant where it all would come together and provide me with the caring conclusion I so desperately sought, stubbornly refused to happen.

So I turned to the trusty fallback plan that had helped me so often over the course of the past six months: I enlisted Mikey's help. Maybe, my thinking went, if I could get Mikey to convince Joe to take me out on his old Noorduyn Norseman float plane— likely the most sentimental plane Joe owns—he would let his guard down and let me in.

I envisioned the moment: Joe and I soar high over Great Slave Lake, the late summer sun casting an orange glow on the land below us. He has decided to take me on a tour of the places that have meant the most to him during his fifty years in the air. We visit Chuck McAvoy's crash site, maybe his old homestead at Gordon Lake. Later that night, as I walk away from the float plane base in front of his Back Bay house, he calls after me and says "Hey! You're not so bad after all."

How wrong I was.

Some aspects of my fantasy held true. Yes, Joe did end up taking me out on the Norseman. That, however, was where any similarity between fantasy and reality came to a crashing end.

THE MORNING OF our long-awaited trip, Mikey and I were sitting in his new Ford F-150 on the ramp outside the Yellowknife hangar, waiting for the sked to arrive from Hay River. It was a Saturday morning, which boded well: if Joe McBryan is going to do anything resembling kicking back and relaxing, it would be on a Saturday or Sunday. But this morning, things started to go wrong right away: there was heavy fog in Hay River, so the sked was delayed three hours. It was almost noon by the time it arrived.

"The sked is delayed only about three times a year," Mikey said, "and never for this long."

Terrific.

Yet despite the weather, Joe was surprisingly upbeat when he got off the plane. As Mikey says, Joe doesn't usually get hung up about things he can't control. And with safety such an important priority for him, Joe McBryan will not risk the well-being of his crew and his passengers for anything. He actually threw me a casual "Hi" as he walked out of the cockpit.

After helping the rampies unload the plane, I wandered into the kitchen, the one place I knew Joe would eventually show up. As usual, Joe was buzzing in and out, holding a conversation with Mikey and me and simultaneously performing some mysterious task in another part of the hangar. It seemed like every time he walked into the kitchen he plunged his hand into the big glass jar of jujubes on the table and deposited a handful into his mouth.

"You can't sit still, can you?" I asked.

"Why would I want to sit still?" he barked at me. "Is it productive to sit still? Might be productive for you, not me." His face, I noticed, had started to turn red.

So I tried to break the ice by asking him a few questions about his past. If I'd come to know anything about Joe, it was that he's a stickler for dates. So even though I knew the answers to the questions I was asking, I threw them out anyway. I figured it may be a way to draw Joe in, open the door to more conversation.

Wrong strategy. As soon as I asked Joe about a couple of dates (in this case, when he started Buffalo and acquired his first DC-3), he used it as an opportunity to lecture me on what the book should and shouldn't contain.

"All you need to say is I learned to fly a DC-3 in Whitehorse in 1969. And by the seventies I was operating them. But if you wanna get date-specific, then..."

He stopped talking for some reason, so I figured it was my chance to jump in and clear the air. "All I really wanted to know was—"

"That's all you have to say: we were into them in the seventies, and we've been operating them ever since. I don't think that's *Star Wars*."

"The historical stuff is pretty brief, I just wanted—"

"I don't wanna get into that," he said. "Because then I have to sit down and do the whole thing. And then it'll just look like a Max Ward book, eh? Now hopefully this book just covers you and Mikey and the Ice Pilots."

"Well, that's most of it, but there is some stuff about you in it and how—"

"Then all you gotta do is say that Buffalo Airways and I came together on May 13 of 1970. You don't have to go into how I got it, why I got it, what I paid for it—all that bullshit."

"That's pretty much all it is, Joe, just a little historical contex—"

"So all you gotta do is say the company's been here since 1970, operating DC-3s since the seventies, and kick-start into the *Ice Pilots*. Mikey can do the rest."

I started to talk again, but Joe would have none of it. He stopped pacing for a second (which was disarming enough) and looked right through me. "I can tell you and I aren't gonna get along," he growled.

Yikes. I was stuck in a real-life version of Groundhog Day, the 1993 movie where Bill Murray is forced to live the same day over and over again for eternity. I knew, *knew,* that any second now Joe was going to say, "Book—what book?"

As always, Mikey came to my rescue. "What about that Norseman flight?" he chimed in.

A COUPLE OF HOURS LATER, the three of us reconnoitred at Mikey's place. I showed up with sandwiches and Timbits in one last desperate attempt to win Joe's favour, but as luck would have it, he'd already eaten.

The Norseman bobbed serenely in the waters behind the house, unmistakable in mustard yellow with highlights of Buffalo green. My original fantasy had me and Joe taking off alone together, but he wanted none of it. Still trying to figure out exactly *why* he was taking me for a ride, he urged Mikey to join us, which he did. Luckily, Joe offered me the right seat in the cockpit; Mikey sat in the back.

CF-SAN

JOE'S Noorduyn Norseman (call letters CF-SAN) boasts a rich history, a litany of owners, and a restoration effort that saw the plane pulled from the scrap heap and knocked back into perfect flying shape once again, courtesy of Buffalo's mechanics.

The plane was registered to Saskatchewan Government Airways (the province's first and only government-owned commercial airline) in 1947. There it flew thousands of kilometres of dedicated service before being damaged in a taxiing accident on June 16, 1960, at Île-à-la-Crosse, Saskatchewan. The plane was salvaged, repaired, and put back into service using parts from another Norseman (call letters CF-EZK). It was sold to Saskair in 1964.

The Norseman was soon bought by Ontario Central Airlines, which operated it until the spring of 1971, when it began a circuitous route through several operators in Manitoba, Ontario, and the Northwest Territories. CF-SAN was damaged again in late 1981, when frost on its wings caused it to crash after takeoff from the airport in Fort Simpson, Northwest Territories.

At that point, CF-SAN's fate hung in the balance. The wreck was shipped to Calgary to be rebuilt, but was deemed beyond repair. So it sat until 1993, when it was donated to the Aero Space Museum of Calgary; Joe bought the wreck later that year. Using parts from Joe's original Norseman (call letters CF-NVJ), which was damaged in the firefighting incident, CF-SAN was rebuilt and registered to Buffalo Airways. Joe flies the plane to this day.

Though I only had the opportunity to fly in Joe's Noorduyn Norseman once, the plane holds a special place in my heart given its rich history in Canadian bush flying. The first recorded flight of a Norseman was on November 14, 1935.

Soon the plane was taxiing across Back Bay. The front of the plane sat so high in the water that it was almost impossible to see over the engine and propeller directly in front of us, but Joe guided the plane masterfully. A few minutes later he turned into position and gunned the engine; the Norseman immediately rode high in the water, its floats skimming lightly across the dark surface of Back Bay. Soon we were in the air, and Yellowknife receded beneath us.

Though he'd done this tens of thousands of times before, Joe was all business behind the Norseman's controls. His hands moved deftly from the yoke to the various switches, buttons, and levers peppered throughout the cockpit. The Norseman did her part too: she was graceful and elegant in the air, and showed no sign of her nearly seventy years. Comforted in the knowledge that I was in good hands, I sat back and enjoyed the ride.

Joe circled around Back Bay and I could see the dichotomy of the city laid out beneath me. From here, a few hundred feet off the ground, it was easy to make out rustic and colourful Old Town, protruding like a jointed finger into the waters of Great Slave Lake. Farther south, the tall buildings of downtown eventually gave way to the sprawl of neighbourhoods to the west of the city's core.

Yet it was the water below that held my attention like a vise grip on this warm and breezy summer day. The many lakes that pepper the cityscape gleamed dark blue beneath us, the warm afternoon sun reflecting off their choppy surfaces. Frame Lake stood out proudly, in some places lined with trees and grass, in others interrupted by a massive, curving, and crevassed outcrop of charcoal-coloured rock. Among the many buildings that line its shore, the Northwest Territories Legislative Assembly is most distinctive; from above it looked like a huge silver-green alien craft waiting for the mother ship to land.

The Norseman was loud—*really* loud—but with the headset on, the sound of the engine died away. Joe, Mikey, and I were able to talk to one another. Mostly, Joe ordered me not to touch any of the controls.

For the next half-hour we flew south, over the waters of Great Slave Lake and past Dettah, an aboriginal settlement of about 250 people that sits across the finger of Yellowknife Bay from the city itself. And if I was expecting to see nothing but the wide expanse of black water in every direction, Great Slave Lake had other plans for me, at least this close to shore. A few hundred feet below us, the water was a hodgepodge of rocky islands. Despite their myriad shapes and sizes, the islands had one thing in common: all were covered in a combination of brown-grey rock and the green of stunted spruce trees. Around the islands, submerged rock cast colourful shadows under the water, from browns and tans to greens and blues.

We weren't the only ones with the idea of exploring the countryside that Saturday afternoon. In almost every direction I turned, boats plied the waters of the lake, leaving foggy fingers of white foam trailing behind. Their destinations eluded me for a while, but as Joe brought the Norseman ever lower, I realized where they were going. Scattered throughout the islands below were signs of occasional human inhabitance: a small cabin here, a canvas wall tent there. Many Yellowknifers are devout outdoorspeople, and those with boats build their camps on the islands in the waters around the city.

Fittingly enough, our destination that afternoon was a fishing camp where one of Joe's friends, Dean, spends time on the weekends. My fantasy of Joe taking me to the places that had shaped his life as a bush pilot had long since vanished, but I was grateful for any opportunity to get up in an airplane with Joe. Plus, meeting someone whom Joe calls a friend—not to mention seeing how Joe operates in a social setting—would be an opportunity I might never get again. In the end, I knew Joe didn't have to do this for me. I imagined he didn't want to, either. But he did it . . . and that says a hell of a lot about the man.

Soon we put the plane down and were taxiing across the water, hoping Dean had seen us and was coming by boat to lead us to his camp. That's when the unthinkable happened. A horrible shrieking noise filled the cabin and we could feel something grinding underneath us. The right side of the plane lifted up slightly, sending us all leaning toward the left. The right float of the Norseman had ground up against a flat, shallow rock.

I looked at Mikey.

Mikey looked back at me.

Joe looked shocked. "Shit," he muttered softly.

We were stuck.

If you're thinking this kind of thing is a common occurrence, think again. Joe says it's only the second time in his life he's ever run aground with a float plane. The last time was in a Cessna 182 with his brother Ronnie. They tore the float right open.

We were luckier today. Everything seemed intact, but that didn't mean we were going anywhere soon. Joe snapped to attention, ordering Mikey and me out of the plane to inspect the damage. Mikey was out before the words were out of Joe's mouth, though; he seems to have inherited his father's ability to handle stressful situations.

By the time I managed to squeeze myself through the plane's tiny side door, Mikey was already standing on the float, assessing the damage. Joe was right behind me. Amazingly, the boss was not angry. He calmly examined the situation, then rubbed his weathered forehead as he decided the best course of action. While I entertained worst-case scenarios like swimming to the nearest fishing camp or diving into the icy water to push the plane free, Mikey spoke.

"Maybe if we stand on the back of the floats it'll raise the front of the plane enough to free us up," he said.

Seconds later, Mikey and I were doing just that, jumping up and down ever so slightly to coax the uncooperative float off the hidden rock shelf. Joe paced up and down the left float, considering his options.

Nothing happened.

Mikey and I kept hopping. Joe kept pacing. Then, just when it seemed like we were going to become more acquainted with Great Slave Lake than any of us had originally bargained for, the aviation gods smiled upon us and sent a blast of cool wind across the lake. That gust, combined with our hopping, set the Norseman free. At the same time, Joe flagged down a passing boat (which turned out to be a friend of Dean's who'd come to escort us to the camp).

Soon the "rock incident" was a distant memory. Joe taxied the plane across the water, slowly following the escort boat to Dean's camp. Mikey had replaced me in the right seat; he was looking for shallow rocks as Joe guided the plane through myriad channels between the innumerable small islands that characterize this part of Great Slave Lake. After about twenty minutes of taxiing, the boat disappeared through a narrow strait.

That was enough for Joe: the passage was just too tight, too shallow, and too risky, so he turned around and headed for open water. He could visit Dean another time. Soon we were back up in the air, circling low over the rocky point of land that marks Dean's camp. A group of people was down there, all looking up and waving at the Norseman. Joe McBryan waved back.

AFTER A BRIEF TOUR over Yellowknife and the surrounding area, Joe brought the Norseman down on Back Bay and turned to me. "Is that what you wanted?" he asked.

"It is, Joe. Thanks."

Rod was waiting for us as we came alongside the dock, ropes ready. I hopped out to lend a hand, but realized that I was intruding on a scene that was never mine in the first place. I watched as Joe, Mikey, and Rod chatted away, father and sons doing what too few of us do, whether it's in Yellowknife or Yemen: pass the time with one another, relishing the simple joy of being together.

For a moment, I was tempted to interrupt them and thank each in turn for the part he has played in helping this book come together. I even started taking a step or two toward the McBryans. Then I stopped, took in the scene one long last time, turned, and walked away.

"You guys wanna go for a ride on the boat?" I heard Joe call out. I knew he wasn't talking to me.

I had a plane to catch.

ACKNOWLEDGEMENTS

On August 20, 2011—shortly after I bade farewell to Yellowknife for the last time while writing this book—a Boeing 737 passenger aircraft operated by First Air crashed on approach to the airport in the tiny High Arctic hamlet of Resolute, one of Canada's northernmost communities. It was foggy that day, but nothing worrisome enough to stop charter flight 6560, which originated in Yellowknife, from redirecting to another airstrip. Twelve of the fifteen people on board were killed.

Little more than four weeks later—as I was putting the finishing touches on this manuscript—a Twin Otter float plane operated by Arctic Sunwest Charters crashed into an empty lot in the Old Town section of Yellowknife as it approached the company's float plane base on Back Bay, not far from Mikey McBryan's house. Returning from a trip to a mining exploration camp at Thor Lake (about one hundred kilometres east of Yellowknife), the plane plowed into a residential street, narrowly missing buildings on either side. The pilot and co-pilot were killed; all seven passengers survived. Nobody yet knows what caused the crash.

Then, unbelievably, disaster struck a third time. On October 4, 2011, an Air Tindi Cessna 208B crashed between Yellowknife and Lutselk'e, a small community some 200 kilometres (125 miles) to the east of the capital. Two of the four people on board, including the pilot, were killed when the plane apparently hit the top of a hill about forty kilometres (twenty-five miles) from its destination.

For me, the foray into the world of bush flying was an ephemeral one. Sure, there were times when I felt like I was living the life of a bush pilot, but I never really did. I tagged along, took people up on their offers of hospitality, flew in some amazing aircraft, told a story. But I never experienced the indescribable feeling of sitting behind the controls, looking onto a landscape of stark northern wilderness, and realizing that something terrible was about to happen. This book is dedicated to anyone who has ever found himself or herself in that position.

If anything, those tragedies made my time in Yellowknife even more important to me. For as I look back, I realize that while the stories of people like Joe McBryan, Justin Simle, Carl Clouter, and Scotty Blue were only ever stories to me, they were white-knuckle real to them. The idea of Carl crash-landing a plane in the High Arctic *sounded* exciting to me, but he *felt* it. It's an important distinction. Having to relive that kind of experience with someone you hardly know cannot be a comfortable undertaking, and I will be forever grateful to those who did. And so, the humble words in these pages are my long-winded way of saying thanks to all of those who let me share their lives, if only for a moment.

Yet for all of those who opened their doors, their memories, and their hearts to me throughout 2011, none deserves more credit than Mikey McBryan. Rain or shine, day or night, –25° or +25°, Mikey was there to help me navigate the sometimes treacherous waters of Buffalo Airways. He took me in, answered thousands of questions about the most intimate details of his life, and never wavered in his commitment to this project . . . even when his dad was on the warpath. Without him, this book would not exist. I'll miss the wings at Surly Bob's.

Then there's Trena White, my confidante at D&M Publishers. Like Mikey, Trena entered my world as a voice on a phone. Over the course of 2011, she has evolved into so much more: friend, advisor, therapist, cheerleader, sounding board, and, of course, editor. If there is anything redeeming about the words in these pages, as much credit is due to her as it is to me.

In the end, a book, like a plane, is the sum of its many parts. This one is no different. So to all the people I am lucky enough to have love me, who put up with my crankiness, my distractedness, and my absence at some point during 2011, I thank you. My name may be on the cover, but the subtext of *Ice Pilots* is all yours.

I don't think that's *Star Wars*.

PHOTO CREDITS